Teenage Morality

Harold Loukes

TEENAGE MORALITY

SCM PRESS LTD

334 01593 6

First published 1973
by SCM Press Ltd
56 Bloomsbury Street London

© SCM Press Ltd 1973

Printed in Great Britain by
Northumberland Press Limited
Gateshead

Contents

1

The Disturbing Generation

It would not be difficult to write a Black Paper about contemporary teenagers, proving them to be set firmly on the road to ruin. We could show how in ten years the male rate for indictable crime has trebled for the years fourteen to seventeen and quintupled for seventeen to twenty-one; while the female crime rate has more than doubled for fourteen to seventeen and trebled for seventeen to twenty-one. Indictable crime, we could be reminded, includes such activities as murder and wounding, rape and indecency, burglary and theft, fraud and forgery, coining, destroying ships (or lightships), obstructing railway engines, and inviting an infant to bet. If the young continue to expand their interest in these activities at the rate they have done of late, then by the year 2000 half the early teenage boys, and all the older ones, will be found guilty, provided their elders have time to catch them.

Or we could tell the story of the overthrow of the tradition of chastity before marriage. At fifteen, two-thirds of the boys are busy kissing and a fifth of them are engaged in deep petting, or more. By nineteen, two-thirds of them are engaged in deep petting, and a half of these are practising full intercourse with more than one partner. Teenage parties are becoming an institution, to cater for other sorts of intercourse than the merely social ('But Mummy, you *must* have three rooms, one for the eats, one for dancing, and one for snogging'). And all round us in the street we see them cuddling on the way home from school, one arm busy with love, the other carrying the little bags of homework.

Or we could, with less measurable evidence but correspondingly more hair-raising power, describe the general relaxation of ideals and hopes. The alarming feature of it all, it is said, is not – not *yet*, they add darkly – the actual changes in behaviour, but the changes in attitude to behaviour. We must judge our situation by what people are now proud or ashamed of doing, by the way the community distributes censure and praise, punishment and reward. By this measure contemporary adolescents are in a bad way. They scarcely ever seem to distribute censure at all, except to those who censure them. They are the thrustful destroyers of tradition, winning from a timorous and permissive society the right to do their own things. Promiscuity is becoming a positive ideal: like many other ideals it is not yet generally practised, but it is being increasingly presented as of virtue in itself, as an alternative to war, as a condition of the growth of the free spirit.

At a slightly less idealistic level, sexual experience is represented as a kind of induction course before the commitment of marriage. Listen to these apprentices discussing their situation.

> Don't you think you've got to look round and probably get the wrong one, you know – you can get an electric shaver on seven days and send it back if you don't like it. You try different ones, don't you, to find out and see if you've got the right one.

> Well, you always find you respect the girl who won't let you more than the girl who will. You'll always find that. If a girl lets you first night, you don't bother with her, but if she won't you keep going with her. You respect her: it's something to conquer.

> Now that's a fact. You find a nice girl, and it's very very rare you touch her. In fact you don't. If you find a girl you really admire and really like, you get a date and you don't touch her. I know from my case I don't.

> That's what I say – respecting her. If you know she's respectable, you don't try anything. And you know if you try summat, she'll slap your face, so that's how you respect her. You keep going with her and going with her, until eventually you get married, and then you get it, you know.

> Another thing. If you have sex-relations with a girl and you get it first night, you think, Well, if she let me have it now, she'll let anybody else have it if they come along. Even when you're married.

> Yes, you can't trust most married men. You can't trust anybody. I mean you've got to chain her to bed. You'll still be sold, though.

It is true this conversation contains a trace of the ancient prejudice in favour of virginity in a bride, but it is not clear where all the virgins are to come from; and it *is* clear that all and sundry are to be subject to trial-by-assault.

In pursuit of their own pleasures, the indictment continues, teenagers increasingly dismiss their parents' wisdom as irrelevant and out of date. They cease to communicate with them on any matter of importance. James Hemming quotes the remarkable story of the girl who wanted to talk to her mother:

> I always talk things over with mummy. Do you think this is strange, because the girls at my school think it is. They say they don't tell their mothers *anything*.[1]

'I don't see,' she added defiantly, 'I don't see why I shouldn't talk to my mother if I want to.' If parents do hear what is going on, and put up opposition, they are routed by an appeal to the teenage culture ('But everybody does it'), or by sheer aggressiveness. 'The bad boy of the past ran away from his parents, the bad boy of to-day intimidates them.'[2] They have no interest in the rituals which make society cohere, they spend their vast income on cheap clothes and pop records, they pursue short-term happiness – and the rare one who notices that it does not work feels himself a stranger to his generation. 'Everything's geared to happiness, these days,' observed a girl sadly, 'and if you don't find it you feel you're a failure.'

We are faced, it is said, by a permissive situation, in which 'anything goes ... a general relaxation of standards, a greater permissiveness, a raising of the demands a man may make on life, and a lowering of the demands life may make on him.'[3] And so, the black story runs, making their demands but accepting none, our adolescents are impossible.

Here are three formulations of the charge, from three widely different sources:

> They have execrable manners, flout authority, have no respect for their elders. What kind of awful creatures will they be when they grow up?

> The young people of today think of nothing but themselves. They have no reverence for parents or old age. They are impatient of all restraint. They talk as if they alone knew everything.

> I do not know whether I deceive myself, but it seems to me that the young men who were my contemporaries fixed certain principles in their minds, and followed them out to their logical consequences in a way which I rarely witness now. No one seems to have any distinct convictions, right or wrong: the mind is completely at sea, rolling and pitching on the waves of facts and experiences.

I conceal the names of the authors for the moment, so that these dark thoughts can make their impact. The contempt for authority and impatience of restraint, the self-centredness, the lack of clear thinking and clear conviction, the sheer immediacy and lack of principle in their behaviour, here surely we have the charge against the contemporary adolescent. These words might any of them have been quoted from letters to *The Times*, the key-note speech at an educational conference, a debate in the House of Lords, or a Black Paper on education. In fact the first quotation is from Socrates, the second from Peter the Monk (in 1274), and the third from Coleridge.

This is the first, perhaps rather simple, but certainly very necessary, point to be made when we contemplate 'Young People Today': that there were Young People Yesterday, who often made their elders cross. Our Young People have, indeed, taken the point themselves. Here are some fifteen-year-old thoughts, arising from a discussion on school punishments.

> The thing I think teachers don't remember, when they give you punishments, is *they* were probably worse. My dad keeps reminding me, he says, Oh you shouldn't do this and that and yet he tells me stories about how bad he was at school and all the things he did at school – they don't remember this when they give you a good hiding or hit you round the ear-'ole.

The second point to be made is equally simple: that the Black Paper can be written in white, the story told, equally plausibly, from another angle. The juvenile crime rate increases fast: but then the rate for men over thirty has doubled, and that for women over thirty more than doubled, in the same ten years. It is true that more young people than old people appear in court, but for most people one appearance in court is enough: they learn from it, and do not appear again. So these youthful appearances function as learning situations, and the young defendants 'learn their lesson', which is more than can be said for many of the older defendants. True, 2·5% of younger adolescents were found guilty of indictable offences in 1969; but then 97·5% were not found guilty. There would, of course, be some guilty ones who were not charged, but at the worst it could be argued, 90% were conducting themselves within the law. And if we recall the increased opportunity for crime – the supermarkets, the streets full of cars, the anonymity of the large town – then we may feel that a rising crime rate is not necessarily a sign of any special corruption in the youthful character.

The figures for sexual adventure can be treated in the same way. True, boys and girls are busy kissing at fifteen, but four-fifths go no further. True, a third of the boys are promiscuous at nineteen, but two-thirds are not, after five or six years of physical maturity. Of the one-fifth of the nineteen-year-old girls who have had intercourse, a half have had it with only one partner. A survey of unmarried mothers of eighteen revealed that three-quarters of them owed their child to a steady relationship. A fifth of all illegitimate births are to teenage girls, but only 1% of single girls in their teens had a child, against 5% of those in the twenties and early thirties (who ought, after all, to have learnt to look after themselves by now). True, the teenage petting-party seems established as a social institution, but its scale is limited, both in number and social class; and even here it may be that a kind of learning goes on, the learning of where you stand. 'You have to decide for yourself, how far you will let them go,' said one girl, 'and then stick to it.' 'How far,' asked a girl at a sex education session, 'how far should you let them go? Is it all right to let them mess about up top?' It may well be that institutions that make this a real question – and it *is* a real question for the developing personality – are institutions not entirely without value.

In choosing whether to print our figures in black or white, most of us will be influenced by our temperament and personal experience. Many statistics are difficult to obtain, and when obtained difficult to interpret, and when interpreted difficult to evaluate. Do we, for example, approve of or deplore kissing at fifteen or intercourse with a 'steady' at nineteen? What is perhaps more formidable in the indictment is the charge that the climate and thought and conversation is now so permissive that corruption must set in. The older generation is accustomed to a climate in which the nasty is shocking, and many would maintain that the shockingness of nastiness is important for its control. A healthy community reacts spontaneously against moral infection just as a healthy body reacts against a virus: the presumed rights of the virus can be discussed after the return to health. The apparent reluctance of the young to be shocked, therefore, means that they have lost a vital defence against disease. It is a short step from not disapproving to approving, and finally to welcoming and seeking out, from saying 'This doesn't matter' to 'Nothing matters'.

Now it must be admitted that there is force in this argument. The media of public conversation, press and radio, screen and stage, do not like the way such arguments make their work more difficult, and so, in public, the side that attracts the attention is the permissive side, as any bishop knows when his largely conventional diocesan letter is ignored while his permissive impromptu is widely quoted.

The conversation of the media thus begins to sound like the conversation of the people, which the young, with their own reasons for accepting it, will come to believe in.

The first question to ask here is a question of fact: *Is* the conversation of the young as permissive as we think? Is it really the case that they are unshockable, that they dream of or hope for, let alone assume, that anything goes? It is clearly impossible to answer this question with complete certainty. A thousand research-workers disguised as teenagers (and for this they would have to *be* teenagers) might perhaps assemble a tolerably valid report, after an exhausting cruise round the school playgrounds and lavatories, the petting parties and youth clubs; but even they would be in the end suspect, for they would import their own impartiality into a situation that might not be impartial at all.

What I have to offer is even more suspect: conversations conducted inside school by a stranger from the generation with whom, it has been said, communications have broken down and war has been declared. Considered as *evidence*, this kind of report has little force. It is hearsay, which no court of justice would be allowed to consider; it is conducted in a situation where young people have learnt to be wary; it is conducted by a visitor approved by the headmaster, talking, inevitably, 'foespeak'.

This is not evidence, in the sense that it proves anything, but I shall hope to show that it is not without a certain illuminating power. It must be treated with due caution, but it cannot be dismissed. For it does, by its very existence, disprove one of the charges that is frequently made: that communications have broken down. Here, in this improbable situation, these youngsters *talked*. It would presumably be possible for the lunatic sceptic to argue that the whole thing is an exercise in deceiving the enemy (for these youngsters, as we shall see, believe in lying in a good cause), but on the face of it, the talk seems sincere enough. If it *is* lying, then they are more skilled in the manipulation of language than their spelling would suggest.

The report that follows tries to answer three questions:

1. How do young people view the moral situation they see themselves in?

2. How do they view the moral guidance they have received in school, and, in particular, do they sense any conflict between home values and school values?

3. What are we to make of it all?

The argument proceeds thus:

1. Chapter 2 presents extracts from conversations which took place on a number of occasions with fifteen-year-old boys and girls in state secondary schools, reported without comment, and with no more editing than is necessary to avoid tedium and irrelevance.

Chapter 3 picks up the main themes of chapter 2, and samples the weight of opinion behind certain of the attitudes displayed in the discussions; and illustrates the range of individual responses.

Chapter 4 links the two sections of reporting together, and directs attention to the area that might be described as moral education.

2. Chapters 5 and 6 are similar in form to chapters 2 and 3, reporting their discussions, and their responses to questions, on their moral education.

3. Chapter 7 considers the significance of their judgment on their moral education, and

Chapter 8 indicates, in general terms, what moral education might in practice mean.

The questionnaire was designed, quite deliberately, as a provocative and not a categorizing device, It *measures* very little, and those who like precise measures will find it unsatisfactory. But there is not much to be gained by seeking precise measures of straws in the wind; and fifteen-year-olds are still so blown about, and tomorrow will be so blown about by other winds, that elegant categories would do very little for our understanding.

To gain immediacy in this object of sensing the windiness, the choices were put before them in their own language, drawn from the discussions. Though I report on the responses in two parts, the questionnaire was in fact administered in one piece; and occupied approximately forty minutes, in a normal classroom situation. Furthermore, though I present the findings in 'graded' order, for ease of interpretation, the questions were arranged in random order.

Then what do they say, as they gather round a tape-recorder in the classroom, or bite their pencils before a questionnaire, answering the strange enemy who questions them about right and wrong?

2

Talking about Morality

1 *The problem of right and wrong*

Five groups of children examine what it means to use the words
'right' and 'wrong'. Are any particular actions always wrong? And
can we agree about what they are? The talk ranges over murder,
and killing in self-defence; and – what they know more about –
lying, lying for a cause, lying for a friend, lying in tact and care for
another's feelings; and also shop-lifting, and whether even this might
sometimes be justified. They conclude with a refusal to accept as
binding any set of 'ten commandments', as being too blunt an
instrument of ethical response; but they equally refuse to give up
the notion that right and wrong mean *something*: petty pilfering
may be only petty, 'but it's wrong though'.

(i) Is there anything at all that you would want to say was always wrong?

> Murdering somebody – killing somebody.

> But somebody you kill might have killed your wife or somebody.
> Then it's not so wrong to kill them back.   (*laughter*)

Well, you may laugh, but this is right up to a point, isn't it? You are
trying to say that some things are 'wronger' than others, that if somebody killed in blind passion, because somebody has killed his wife, it
is not as bad as a cold-blooded, plotted murder.

> I'd say it's still the same, because it's taking somebody's life,
> isn't it?

Yes, but he didn't really *think* of taking somebody's life.

> Yes, but look, suddenly this person kills another person, right,
> and then you go and take his life, right, then that's still taking
> two lives instead of one. It's different if the courts sentence him
> to death because they've got the jurisdiction to do it. I don't see

why somebody should take it into their own head and just go off and kill somebody. (*cries of disagreement*)

Are you saying that you have a list of offences which are always just totally black, and can't be forgiven?

No, but you were on about the case of murder, and murders are always the same kind.

Well, OK then. What if an assassin creeps up on somebody and kills them for their money – don't you think that's more wrong than someone in a fight who hits him too hard and kills him?

That's not murder, that's manslaughter.

It is *not*.

It is. It could be self-defence.

Could I put up another sort of issue? One of the broad moral rules that we go by is that we speak the truth most of the time. Now does this come under your sort of rule? You are saying that murder is always wrong. Would you say that lying is always wrong?

Well, there's a lie that doesn't really matter. It's a lie and that's it. You're protecting a friend, say, and then there's another lie, and you really mean it ... I can't explain it ... You're protecting yourself, and the other lie you're talking about is just a fib, you might say, in the heat of the moment, just to get a friend out of trouble. There's another lie just to protect yourself.

Now this is very interesting. You are advancing the *test* as being, Is this done for myself or for somebody else? Would you be wanting to say that the only kind of ten commandments you would accept would be commandments like, Thou shalt put other people's interests before your own?

No, no. It's not what I'm saying. I'm saying it's a *small* lie, that doesn't have any consequences, which doesn't matter at all. I mean, you take an apple off a tree and you say you never took it. I mean there's nothing wrong with that, is there?

Ah, so what you are doing is setting up a grading system, is it? You want to ask, Is this a whopping lie or is it a small lie? And small lies are right? Is that it?

It's a small lie until you say that somebody else took it. And as soon as you say somebody else took it, it's a big lie.

But how does that make it a *big* lie?

Because you're getting somebody else into trouble. You're putting yourself before somebody else. You're getting yourself out of trouble by getting somebody else into it.

So you're really accepting my suggestion about a new commandment, that as long as you're doing something on behalf of somebody else, you may be justifiable.

It's right; but it's something everybody should come to themselves. It shouldn't be a commandment, that is put down by one person that everybody has to keep to.

If you're lying for a cause, and you believe in it ...

So you don't mind politicians doing it?

Oh, politicians ... politicians are perfect examples of grown-up babies. They are just sitting there thinking something and they start up to say something or other as if they've just thought of something, and whatever one side says the other has to disagree with.

Yes, even if it goes against their beliefs.

(ii) Is it always right to tell the truth? and always wrong to tell a lie?

No, I reckon it's partly right to tell a lie – if you're defending someone, and you really like that person then it's natural to tell a lie to defend him. If you tell the truth, then that person will have a grudge against you and he's bound to get his own back on you.

If you tell a lie, the person you're telling a lie to usually finds out it's a lie and that doesn't help the person you're defending.

You think it wise, and common sense, to tell the truth, so you won't be found out?

Well, if you tell a lot of lies people won't believe you when you tell the truth.

Lying on behalf of somebody else, is this 'good'?

Well, it would all depend on why he's lying – what he's lying about. If this bloke had killed a man, and his friend liked him a lot and defended him – there might be something wrong with this man – there might be emotional strain.

Well, say you have a friend in school, and he's done something wrong, do you cover up for him or do you tell?

If it's your friend, you *do* cover up.

Now would you think this is an unfailing rule, or is there any qualification to it?

> If he did it accidentally, then I think I'd definitely cover up for
> him, but if he did it deliberately and he did harm to some-
> one ...

Would you also not think it's something to do with the seriousness of
what he's up to? If he'd drawn a funny picture of one of the staff
on the blackboard, then it doesn't matter very much. But if he'd killed
someone, would you then cover up?

> I think inwardly we would like to, but if this man is loose he
> might kill somebody else and then somebody dies because of this
> man not saying anything.

The next person might be yourself.

(iii) Many of you will presumably one day be bringing up children.
Would you like them to tell the truth?

> Yes.

Always?

> (*Voices*) Yes ... No ... Yes

> Not if the truth will hurt somebody else. I mean Aunt Molly comes
> along with a stupid great big hat and the children think it's funny,
> you don't want them to say, Oh look at Aunt Molly, doesn't she
> look silly in that great big hat?

> I don't think that's telling lies: I think that's really tact.

> I don't think people trust in each other. If people trusted in each
> other then they'd get on better with each other and speak the
> truth.

You make a distinction between telling the truth and tact. So would
you say that what we might call little lies, saying Oh yes, I do like
your dress – these don't matter?

> No, that's being tactful. If you say you don't like their dress, that's
> hurting them, you see; and it's better to be tactful.

So this has a general rule behind it, has it, that people's feelings are
more important than telling the truth?

> Yes, I think so.

> But if you don't like somebody's dress, you don't have to say
> you like it. You can just keep your mouth shut.

So you would not always want your own children to be truthful?

> On the major issues I would like them to be truthful. But over just little things which would hurt other people, I think a white lie is often better than causing hurt.

> I think I'd like my children to be truthful to me. I mean, my mother asks me, Do you like my new dress, and she asks me, you know, for judgment. Not for praise.

> I wouldn't like my child to be a telltale. You know, if he came home, if I asked him what he had been doing today, and it's something naughty, I wouldn't want him to tell on somebody else.

But suppose this friend of your child's were doing something harmful – shoplifting or on drugs or ...

> Oh, I don't mean that sort of thing. I mean at the younger stage.

> But if he doesn't tell you little things then, when he's older he's not going to tell you the truth. Because he's got into the way of it.

> Much as I think the truth is important in our society, you *need* to lie, in many cases. In small matters, and sometimes in larger ones. In politics. They may not actually lie, but they exaggerate and perhaps tell untruths for the good of the nation and things like that.

Would you say that this is necessary?

> In some cases, yes. It's difficult to draw the line, isn't it?

> What I tend to do is not to lie, but to *bend* the truth. Angle it to make it sound good. I wasn't *quite* in the wrong, you know.

Would you think well of yourself for bending ...?

> No, I wouldn't, but I'd think better of myself than lying directly.

> I haven't got a conscience, then. You know, when I just leave bits out or someone has got the impression that I haven't done wrong, even though I have, in my heart of hearts I might feel a bit guilty, but, you know, I go away with a clear conscience, even though I did leave bits out.

Conscience, is this the guide to what to do and what not to do? If we tell an absolute whopper, our feelings tell us, or don't they?

> Yes.

> Sometimes it doesn't help to own up to what you've done, once

you've done wrong. I mean, just going into a room you shouldn't, or doing something that you shouldn't. Then, you just shift the worry on to somebody else. You may just as well keep quiet about it, and if you feel bad about it just not go and do it again.

So again you'd be saying, It's other people who are what make us make decisions about right and wrong?

A lot of people lie to save their own skin, not for other people. And they get to tell big lies, and cause a lot of trouble. And then they just forget all about it.

(iv) Would it be possible to draw up a kind of modern Ten Commandments? Would you be able to say, Now these are the things I would say Thou shalt or Thou shalt not, to somebody of the modern world?

I still like the other Ten Commandments. They still apply. You know, you just look at the Bible and it still applies to the modern world. You just change it slightly.

And if you did start writing a new Ten Commandments I think you'd soon go back to the old ones. They'd still be the same.

Yes, they sort of cover everything.

I think the Ten Commandments are impossible. If you say you want to be good you've got to know the Ten Commandments then I'm just a rotten person.

Impossible to keep up to, do you mean?

M'm. Yes.

I think if you had a new sort of Ten Commandments there'd be a lot more sidetracks to it – like killing in self-defence or in war – this wasn't said in the old commandments.

So how does one *do* this, these days? So far we've been saying that the old commandments were all right, but need qualification. Then how does one do the whole business of thinking out right and wrong? Is there anything actually that you would think was always wrong?

To take a life.

I don't think so. If someone was going to shoot you how would you feel? It's the same thing, isn't it? It's a life for a life.

Can we make any sort of rules, then? You should tell the truth unless ... ?

When you're younger you should tell the truth. It's when you get a bit older when your problems start arising.

Why?

> Well, you come up against more situations, different situations.

> I don't agree. When you're younger, say about ten, and your friend's doing something that's getting him into trouble, you think, 'How to cover up this problem?' It would be wrong, but that's what you'd think of doing. So if you told them not to lie they wouldn't listen to you.

> It depends on who you were. If you were a parent and told them not to lie, I don't think they would lie.

> It depends if they respect you.

> The thing is at that age, if you're not going to say 'Don't split on a friend – ' it might be better not to split on a friend if he did steal something because it might help him. It's not going to get him anywhere. If you split on him when he was young, and the truth comes out, it might stop him from stealing again.

But honestly, if your best friend had done something, would you tell?

> Ah, it's difficult there, isn't it?

> You'd certainly lose your friendship, wouldn't you?

> But what you should do and what you think you should do are different, often, when it comes to doing it.

> And often you wouldn't have time to think over it anyway – should I tell or shouldn't I?

Yes, that's a real question, isn't it? When it comes to choosing between right and wrong, would it be your experience that you do think it out before you act?

> No, we don't have time to do it. At that moment you have to decide.

> It depends on what the situation is. You might have plenty of time.

Yes, this is true, of course. But my guess is that as you go through life you suddenly find you've done something – let down a friend or what have you – without having thought it out at all. Would you think this is right?

> I think you should think about it first.

> Yes, you should think about it a lot, before you let him down, and maybe ask other people's views on the subject.

Yes, you don't want it on your own back all the time – you want to know what other people would do.

But if one of my friends stole something I couldn't go to somebody else and say, Oh she's stolen something, should I tell?

I'd approach him myself first.

I think I'd go to my friend and tell him to go and put the thing back. I wouldn't go and tell someone else.

This would depend very much on what sort of thing we are talking about. Suppose you saw a friend getting hooked on heroin, then you wouldn't mind, presumably, going to someone else and saying, 'Look, this chap's on heroin, can't we help him?' Presumably one has a range of important and unimportant.

I think the biggest is people stealing things, really.

Would you think that stealing things that aren't too serious doesn't matter?

It's wrong, though. I mean it can lead to bigger things.

(v) What about something that comes quite close to us all these days – what about shoplifting? Is it wrong?

Yes.

'Course it is.

M'm ... No, might not be.

Depends.

I mean, if you say you and your friend have been kicked out of your house, have no money, no job, nothing, and you're slowly starving to death, well, you go and nick something, to stay alive. If you had enough food, you know, and just went and nicked it to be big, *then* get a real big punishment. But nicking to stay alive, well, no, not really.

Once you start taking things you're gonna build up to be a big criminal.

I don't know. Suppose you start off at five or six, which people do – mothers and fathers train their children to shoplift – then you're bound to grow up, you know, into the trade.

That's all you know – you're put inside and you come out and that's all you know.

When you're young, you're bound to remember it. It's the best time to be taught something.

Once a person's been inside, he comes out and tries to keep a straight path instead of going back to his old trade, but can't go straight for long – he just doesn't know anything else, anyway.

What's actually wrong with shoplifting, though? Why is it wrong?

It's depriving other people of their right to their property.

But suppose you said to yourself, Oh, Woolworth, silly old blighter, millionaire. And poor old me, haven't even got a pen to write with. What's wrong with that argument?

You could save up for a pen, but if you're starving with no food at all, well, by the time you've saved up to get some money to buy the food, you might be dead.

If you steal something from Woolworth's they'd miss it.

If everybody did that ...

Pennies mount up into pounds, they say.

If you were the person that owned it you'd think of it in a different way. You'd soon put somebody inside for nicking something of yours.

If someone was just about to go into a shop and do some shoplifting, if they thought what it was like to be the person who's losing all the money, then I don't think half of them would do it. Because if they thought of themselves, the manager's losing a lot of money because people shoplift, I don't think they'd do it.

Some people don't like asking for charity.

2 Mercy-killing

Hard cases, we say, make bad laws. Then how do good laws, like the law of the sacredness of human life, work when they encounter hard cases? What are we to say of the mercy-killing of the old, or of a baby born with crippling handicaps? Few of us have to face these questions with the need to make a decision; but they are testing questions, searching out our deepest beliefs about life and the rules within which life is lived.

What do you do with old folk when they get past being able to enjoy life? Eskimos, we are told, when their people get old, leave them out in the snow somewhere. Here we keep them going. But the question is now beginning to be asked, whether – when somebody is frail and in so much suffering that life isn't likely to be worth living any more – whether we shouldn't quietly put them to sleep. Would you like to talk that one out?

(*Pause*)

Does it shock you?

(*Voices*) Yes ... M'm ... Yes

Well, good, that's a good thing to feel first. But on the other hand think of somebody of, say ninety-five, who has become really a vegetable, but medicine is so wonderful today that we can keep her going, just lying in bed, for another five years ... Does that shock you too?

(*Voices*) Oh yes ... yes.

You're overdoing it ... You're just old. You're not enjoying life, perhaps, as other people want you to, but you know, you're all happy and that. It's silly not to keep them ... I mean, you only have one life.

It's up to the person concerned.

But suppose they are past deciding?

But you couldn't say to somebody, Do you want to die, or do you want to sleep, now could you, really?

If somebody does actually say to a doctor, Look, for heaven's sake, finish me off today?

No, that would be killing people.

If he asked the doctor to kill him off that would be committing suicide.

But if you want to die you can die – it's up to you. It's no one else's life. They can't keep you alive if you want to die.

Let me ask about the other end – handicapped babies. If a baby arrives, and it's severely handicapped, would you kill it?

If it's going to live for a long time, if it's going to survive itself, I don't think they should do that, because I don't think it's right.

Then they should say to the parents, I can't do anything about it, then the parents can decide.

A baby was born, once, and the doctor said, If the mother sees the baby it'll shock her so she'll never be the same again. So he killed it.

And do you approve of this?

Well, I dunno.

Well, say this handicapped child, its mind has completely gone, and it won't even have the energy to do anything but lie there for the rest of its life; if they say it died at birth, the mother won't be quite so shocked as if ...

Yes, she didn't even know ... they told her it was a perfectly normal baby, so she thought she was all right.

3   *Drugs*

Our fifteen-year-olds, with their newly-granted freedom of movement, have nothing but their own sense to protect them as they seek, very properly but very dangerously, to find out what excitements the world has to offer them. Here two groups look at the drug problem, with, we might think, a cool eye and a healthy resistance.

(i) Could I raise another sort of question? Let me ask about the drug problem. Do you think this is a moral problem?

In what sense do you mean moral?

Well, deciding whether to take drugs or not: is it a matter of right and wrong?

It's up to you, isn't it?

Yes, it's up to you.

It's the same as smoking. If you want to smoke it's your fault. Smoking a hundred years ago was as harmful as drugs are today, and perhaps in a couple of hundred years time drugs will be an everyday thing.

I think taking drugs is all right as long as you don't try to persuade somebody else to take them, because if you decide personally to take drugs then it's up to you, but if you decide to persuade one person in a group who doesn't then they feel left out, like 'I'm not a member of the group because I don't take drugs,' and that's wrong.

So the only wrong thing is persuading others?

> No, when you take drugs you don't become yourself, you become another person. And you affect the community.

In what way?

> Well, you could obviously persuade them to take it as well. So once you've taken it you persuade them to take the drugs as well, and change them.

But suppose you *don't* persuade somebody else, can you see any point at which this question becomes a question of right and wrong?

> I think it's wrong if it does you any harm.

> What right have the police to stop you taking drugs? Or anybody?

Well, I'm really asking you this one. Suppose we decide that Bertie isn't going to persuade anybody else, but he decides to take heroin. Could he be faulted here? Has society any right to interfere with him?

> No, as long as he doesn't affect society.

But *does* he affect society?

> (*Voices*) No ... no ...

> Not as long as he doesn't give it to anybody else. If he gets somebody to get them for him, then that person gets into trouble. But if he keeps it to himself, then that's not wrong.

> Yes it is. Suppose they're going to kill themselves with drugs, then it's a poison inside you, and if you're having a baby ...

> No, a baby hasn't got a mind of its own yet.

> Yes, but even if it's got a mind of its own, more intelligent people can see what's going to happen, see.

> Yes, but people don't usually take drugs till fourteen or fifteen, and by then it's considered in this day and age that they're old enough to make their own decisions.

> But if it's going to kill them, somebody's got to stop them.

> All right – you stop them building automobiles – *they* kill people.

> I would.

> You would? Go on then, you try to do it. Anyway, that's their job – you're just killing millions of people because they haven't

got food and they're not earning the wages to feed their family. No, this is terrible. Just think what it's going to do.

(ii) But what about the drug situation? The position is that there are one or two drugs like tobacco and alcohol that are permissible – they're under legal control, with rules about who can buy them and when, but they are accessible. But there are certain other drugs which are not accessible, and are very much forbidden. Now does this raise in your mind a problem?

You mean cannabis and that?

Yes.

Well, cannabis and hash are lethal, aren't they? Tobacco and alcohol, perhaps they're lethal, but not for twenty years.

And there's many drugs in hospitals.

Ought we to make cannabis legal?

No. I say hash and pot and things like that should not be made like tobacco and drink. There's a case where this sixteen-year old boy – *he* was on cannabis, and he thought he could fly. So he jumped out of a six-storey building.

The thing is, people who are on drugs, you can't just stop them like that, they sort of have to be weaned off of them. They have to be taken down, in kind of grades.

Another thing is that you can get so much money out of them. They don't care what happens to the people who take them, as long as they can get some money.

So you want to draw a distinction between somebody who takes drugs himself and somebody who pushes them on to other people?

The pusher should get more, when he gets caught and has a sentence, than the person who takes the drugs. The person who takes the drugs is usually conned into doing it.

You don't object that you aren't allowed to buy it for yourselves?

What would I wanna buy it for?

We know what's happened to other people, so why should we want to buy it?

There was this girl, she was dependent on drugs. Then she had this baby, and it was born dependent on them too.

4 *A good person*

If right and wrong cannot be determined by rule, then how are we to recognize it in life? Are there models to which we can point, and say, 'Yes, that is what I mean by right'? These four groups try to establish the idea of the 'good' person, and find this as difficult as agreeing on a moral rule. In particular they are caught in the tension between 'being yourself', with spontaneity and enjoyment, and a little self-indulgence, and 'being for others', with some self-denial, and a certain aloofness from the life of the group. And if you *do* believe in 'being for others', how do you hold on to your values in a materialistic society?

(i) What sort of person would you describe as a *good* person?

> Somebody doing something they were happy doing, that they were good at, not doing something they didn't want to do.

> Changing things ... trying to change things and make them better.

In what direction is better?

> Change it to make less poverty, and make it easier for people to live.

(ii) What sort of qualities would you say that you admire in people? That you would on the whole like to have for yourself? (*Long silence*) ... Let's see if we can get at it another way. Are there any people, either famous people or people that you know yourselves, that you particularly admire?

> Cliff Richard.

Good. Now why is this?

> Because he's established ... and he's written two books ...

> I think I'd admire someone who's an individual, because I think our age now is in with the mass – what it's 'in' to do. I admire anybody who doesn't have to do the same as everybody but stands out on their own.

(iii) If I were to say 'he was a *good* man', what sort of person would you think of?

> A good man, I takes it, well he's got a posh car or something, nice wife, couple of kids, and he don't drink, don't go to Bingo

or anything like that. And he don't smoke, and you never hear him swearing or anything like that.

That's your picture of a good man, is it? And you approve of him? Would that be agreed?

No – a good man isn't – no, what he just said – the picture of a good man in his mind is a goody goody. But a good man, in my mind, is really when a man tries everything, and experiments, and learns by his own judgment, by his own mistakes.

Now tell me something more about what you'd expect him to *be*. At the moment you've just said 'somebody who tries everything for himself'. But I still don't recognize how he would end up – suppose after ten years of trying for himself, what would he be like after that?

Well, I think he would be wise.

Delicate in his doings.

What do you mean by 'delicate'?

In everything he does.

He doesn't want to cause trouble to anybody else. He's careful of what he says.

He's a patient, understanding bloke. He's always willing to have a conversation and then help people and that.

To help others.

Do you know anybody that you would say, Yes, when you ask me that question about what's a good man I think of old so and so?

Yes, I know a bloke just like that. Comes from Harwell.

So you are changing your mind, are you? You don't want your posh-car-and-non-smoking-non-swearing chap, and now you're saying 'somebody who can listen sympathetically to somebody else?' You're voting for Character Two and not Character One, is that right?

No, I was putting them all together. This bloke I'm talking of, he's the actual bloke I'm looking up to.

Who do you want to be *yourself*? This Jag-owning person, or one who listens sympathetically?

Listening to other people.

(iv) Do you think our society would be better were it less materialistic?

(*Voices*)   Yes.

Yes, there's jealousy and things. But you can't get rid of material things. You can't say what it would be like without them.

You can.

You can still say you *think* it'd be better without them.

We know, don't we, that some of us spend an awful lot of time thinking about and wanting possessions. Why do we want them? Are we being selfish?

I think having what we want causes an awful lot of jealousy. And there are people less fortunate than us who can't have what they want. A friend has a new dress and it catches their eye and they want one and they can't afford it. They might go into a shop and shoplift. They want a dress like their friend.

I *like* material things. I like having a nice warm fire to turn on. I work on a farm at weekends, and it gets so cold and so damp and so miserable, and you can't get out of it. And you come home and you really enjoy it. But I went up to Scotland and I met a Scottish girl there, and she knew some crofters and they lived just in two rooms, right up in the Highlands, and she said she'd never met anybody happier.

It's all very well to say you'd be happier without possessions, but you've *got* them, and you've got a material body, and it's the only way you can express your feelings. Material things are very important.

Having had them, you'd miss them, because you'd want them.

But p'raps if you hadn't had them in the first place you wouldn't yearn for them.

Do you feel that sometimes one is not being the version of oneself one would prefer, because one has become too much concerned with material possessions, and one would have a different kind of happiness?

Yes, I think society changes you a lot. People aren't allowed to be what they really are.

Do the rest of you agree with this, that society doesn't let you be who you really are?

I think it's entirely up to you. You can be if you want to be. People are afraid to be themselves. It's a very pretentious society anyway. But you can be completely yourself if you're willing to take the consequences. Which you may or may not.

What *is* being yourself? I mean, who are you? Who really knows what they're like?

I think that is an unanswerable question. But I think one can at times know that one is not being oneself. One feels, not necessarily unhappy, but just not right, perhaps.

You change when you're with different people. You don't have to. You just find yourself adjusting to be with who you're with. Also, you're much more tolerant of people that you like than people that you don't. You just find this, you can't help it.

3

Thinking about Morality

What we have in the last chapter is a record of conversations conducted in peculiar, and seriously restricting, circumstances. They went on in classrooms – and secondary school classrooms are still curiously dismal places. They went on not merely in the presence of a stranger, but under fairly continuous prodding from the stranger. Occasionally the children rounded on each other and began to show their own paces, but even at each other's throats they conducted themselves with classroom decency, with none of the 'no-you-silly-idiots' with which they might argue alone. The stranger tried to be untendentious, but schoolchildren are adept in the knowledge of what is acceptable in an adult presence, and faced by a stranger are endearingly anxious to please. Even a new teacher is offered an ordeal by flattery before the true ordeal begins: as one girl put it, 'When we try out a new teacher we're ever so ever so good until we know what they're like. Then if they're unfair, they're for it.'

Such conversations, then, probably represent children's thoughts at their most accommodating. They are not to be judged positively insincere, but they may well represent only part of the story, for all kinds of suppression occur in such a situation. The less fluent ones do not take part at all, and who can tell what dark thoughts go on within the minds of the silent ones? Even the fluent talkers may have doubts, and temptations to doubts, that they keep out of the public view. They have, as Browning put it, 'two soul-sides, one to face the world with', and the other to be discovered only in rare moments of deep intimacy.

This does not invalidate the conversations as clues to the shape of the adolescent morality, but it does require that we listen to them with caution. They let us, I believe, inside their minds; but not inside the whole of their minds; and hardly at all inside their wills. We still need to know how many of them adopt one or other of the moral postures here outlined, and how many of them would, under the pressure of events, actually stand by their beliefs. Is it merely the fluent ones who deal so smoothly with shoplifting and drugs? And would any of them refuse a dare in Woolworth's or a whiff at a pot-party?

This last question is impossible to answer. Nobody is going to indulge in shop-lifting if he is watched by an army of researchers, and as many adults ruefully know, there is more to giving up smoking than a sincere affirmation of intention.

To the first question, however, some sort of answer can be given from the responses to a questionnaire filled in with time for thought and space for individual comment. Questionnaires, too, must be worked in the classroom, but working alone at his desk a child feels he is in a private place, on his own, anonymous, subject to no conscious pressure towards a particular point of view. The questionnaire that was used was couched in the language of the discussions, so that the suggestiveness of the language itself should at least be teenage suggestiveness. And the questions were designed with a deliberate openness, seeking not precise categories or critical choices so much as clusters of response.

The pupils were given time for thought, but not for long thought. They could give reasons for their choices, but could not engage in elaborate qualification or subtle discrimination. The thoughts that emerge are thus first thoughts rather than second thoughts: they indicate stances but not the depth of argument. They may be said, then, to be an airing of prejudices rather than skill in moral reasoning. But prejudices constitute for most of us the bulk of our moral furniture: they tend to be what we *act* by, whatever may happen when we later scrutinize our actions. It is important, then, to know what they are. At the point of action, it may matter more to know *what* people think than *how* they think.

The articulation of a total moral ideology would prove a complex, and perhaps unnecessary task; so the areas selected for exploration were limited to a few illustrative issues and to some examination of the notion of a 'good person'.

The issues were chosen for familiarity and relative simplicity. Lying, shoplifting and drugs are suitable, because they are very much part of the teenage scene, either in experience or exhortation. Mercy-killing is not, but it is an issue on which public opinion is reasonably clear, and the law is specific. Some issues, perhaps of greater importance, are not easy to explore in this way. War and purposeful violence are more difficult than at first may appear, and demand a range of considerations beyond the power of boys and girls. Sex, which for many people is where the notion of morality begins and ends, is not to be handled by such a blunt instrument as a classroom questionnaire. The public view on sex is now under revision, and difficult to state; even the law, on such a matter as the age of consent, is under attack; and adult opinion on what is desirable, possible to secure, undesirable-but-permissible, revolting, dangerous or unmentionable is so varied and uncertainly held that even asking questions becomes a kind of dreaming.

Let us turn, then, to what they say, in the privacy of the desk and sheet of paper, in answer to this little sample of probing questions.

1 *The problem of right and wrong*

Is there any sort of action you would want to say was always wrong?

> Killing somebody.   A ☐

> But somebody you kill might have killed your
> wife or somebody. Then it's not so wrong to
> kill them back   B ☐

Tick which you prefer.

Can you think of up to five things you would say were always wrong?

———————————————————————

———————————————————————

Would you say that lying is always wrong?

> No.

Then what do you say about it?

> Well, there's a lie that doesn't really matter. There's little lies and big lies. Little lies are just fibs.

> You're protecting a friend, say, that's just a fib; and there's *lies* when you're protecting yourself.

> No there's small fibs to protect yourself. I mean you took an apple off a tree and you say you never took it. I mean there's nothing wrong with that is there? But as soon as you say somebody else took it, it's a big lie.

Do you think lying is   never wrong   ☐
                        sometimes wrong   ☐
                        always wrong   ☐

Why?

These two quotations were displayed to raise the same question: Is it possible to label an action as a wrong action in any circumstances? And if so, what kind of action can be so labelled? And if not, how does one attach meaning to the word 'wrong'? The boys and girls are being asked to display their skill in casuistry, the examination of particular cases in which general moral laws are in apparent conflict with one another. Without casuistry, we should say, general moral laws are dangerous things to follow: but it must be done on principle or it destroys the moral law itself. What is being asked here, then, is, Have you cottoned on to the broad principles of casuistry? Can you do it morally and not just fancifully? The respondents were asked to group themselves according to their belief that killing and lying are always, sometimes, or never wrong (except that they were not offered a choice of saying that killing is never wrong: there is a limit to the idiot questions one can ask, even in a questionnaire).

The results can be given diagrammatically thus:

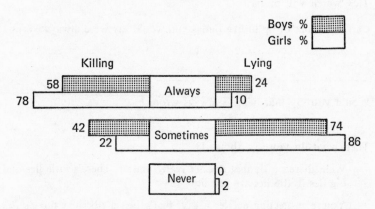

If we ignore the eccentric 2% (all girls, alas) who think lying can never be wrong, we have here an interesting picture of a group of people who have, indeed, grasped the need for casuistry, but have not been adequately trained in its use. The majority are ready to examine cases in the field of lying, but not in the field of killing.

We might hazard two reasons for this: in the relative seriousness, and the relative remoteness of the two sorts of action. Killing, after all, *is* more serious than lying. We would rather be lied to than killed; and the threat of death is more deeply disturbing than the threat of deception. The mere thought of it arouses a kind of shock that makes rational examination difficult, and though the qualification the children were asked to choose ('It's not *so* wrong') is rationally defensible, we can understand that our infant casuists are not ready to run the apparent risk of destroying this crucial moral principle. 'Casuistry destroys,' says Bolingbroke, 'by distinctions and exceptions, all morality'; and there are some principles so important and so emotionally loaded that we can sympathize with a refusal to submit them to examination. That this motivation played some part may be borne out by the fact that while the boys voted only 3:2 for the absolutist position, girls voted 4:1. Boys are still, in our culture, less averse to killing than girls.

The other motive arises from the relative remoteness of killing as an actual event. These children have no experience of killing: they have frequent experience of lying. If we wanted casuistry on killing, we should need to assemble people who have done it or ordered it to be done: soldiers and hangmen and doctors and judges. But lying is a different case. These young people have no intention of destroying the morality here, for, as we have seen, they deplore and are puzzled by lying in general. But they have done it and heard it done, and they are willing to find special labels, such as tact, for special cases. Here, incidentally, the girls are marginally more casuistical than the boys, 86% saying 'sometimes', as against 74% of the boys. But then, girls are more tactful.

Boys and girls alike have difficulty in drawing the line, or at least defining the line in words. One or two cling to a general rule:

> Do not lie is not one of the Commandments but it is nearly just as bad as stealing or killing, if you lie to protect someone you are instantly involved and apart from commiting a sin you will be stopping someone from a just punishment, lying to protect yourself is always wrong.

His shakiness on the Commandments adds point to what the boy said about the difficulty of being good if that required knowing them; but in any case other children advance a counter-rule drawn from social norms:

> Everybody lies anyway.

The world would be CHAOS if everyone always told the truth.

Equally indeterminate is an appeal to expediency. Short-term expediency is often in favour of lying,

> Because sometimes you could be in situations where you need to lie. If you were being threatened then you might tell a lie to get out of it.

> Because you may have to lie to a certain extent to get on in the world. If you didn't want to go out with a friend, you'd say yes but then didn't want to go a lie about saying your ill etc isnt all that bad as other lies people tell you.

And certain situations demand such expediency.

> Necessary in a good cause.

> In war.

> They tell lies in some hospitals about serious conditions that can never be cured.

But the expediency principle raises doubts in the long term.

> It really does help to Lye sometimes but only sometimes, Because it becomes a habit and is done on an increasing scale.

This creeping habit may catch you unawares.

> When you ly you may just change it about, then another time you might change everything, this would be very bad in court.

It is for this reason, some say, that lying is always wrong,

> because you start with a little lie at first but gradually your lies will get bigger and Bigger until you would be lying all the time.

And then where are you?

> You Alway get caught.

The last word rests, perhaps, with those who are drawn to the absolutist position, but find themselves lying nevertheless:

> I wish I knew why – but I don't I just do it without thinking what I'm doing and so do a lot of other people.

So far all that has emerged is the fruit of teaching that any mis-representation is to be called 'lying', and lying is wrong. And so these puzzled youngsters waver between the two impossibilities, of lying but remaining credible, and of truth-telling all the time. But others, easily a majority, offer two positive ways through the muddle.

One is to draw a distinction between situations where it does not matter and those where it matters supremely. There is joke-lying:

> When you are lying to keep a surprise you sometimes need to lie, so that it still remains a surprise.

This, presumably, includes parents telling about Santa Claus, who certainly cannot complain about this lesson being learnt. Or there is compassionate lying:

> Sometimes it is better for someone never to know the truth (what her dead son was. A Killer).

> Lies are alright if you are protecting the feelings of someone else in this sence I do not mean telling a lie if your friend has done something wrong because he ought to be punished but a lie which tell a person who is very ill and has leg cut off that he's leg's alright because the shoch might kill him is alright.

Here we might wonder what sort of a 'shoch' awaits the victim when he discovers, as surely he soon will, not only that he has lost a leg, but that his friend is a liar. But others push firmly forward to the principle that one can lie boldly on behalf of a friend:

> You can lie for protecting a friend or someone you can just bluff for fun ... these are small lies, fib, but when you say that it sone one els did it that would be very wrong.

> Sometimes you have to protect other people and their feelings. But I think you shouldn't lie to protect yourself, this is a coward's way out.

Here they firmly ally themselves with E. M. Forster, who in *The Hill of Devi* wrote: 'If I had to choose between betraying my country and betraying my friend, I hope I should have the guts to betray my country.' And indeed, say some, this is not betrayal, or lying, at all:

> you say it won't be a lie, to protect someon.

Here, of course, we reach a point when we are engaging merely in linguistic quibbling, and casuistry takes on its pejorative sense: the area of lies and fibs, little lies and big, white lies, tact, and the rest. Conducted rigorously this is genuine moral thinking, conducted sloppily it is evasion of thought.

Let us end this discussion with a remark from a boy who seems to occupy the ground on which most boys and girls, and perhaps most adults, would operate, holding an unresolved tension between moral relativism, adjustment to the norm, linguistic distinction, and yet the firm belief in a genuine morality between persons:

> Well what I think is that everybody lies or fibs sometimes in their life, and I don't think it is wrong. When the blame is put on someone else who did not do it that sort of lie is terrible.

What emerges clearly from all this is that these youngsters have grasped the notion that general moral propositions are difficult to maintain, and that 'always wrong' is a difficult thing to say. It is interesting, therefore, to discover that when they are asked for examples of conduct that they would consider always wrong, they ignore the problem, and leap cheerfully to the attack on a wide range of activities. Killing comes predictably high on the list, often under such names as murder or assassination, which carry built-in moral judgments – the philosopher would say that the word 'murder' means 'a-form-of-killing-of-which-we-disapprove'. Then, also frequently mentioned, are forms of violence, such as torture, rioting, 'vandiluzum' (particularly 'being vandles for fun'), baby-snatching, and public violence in the form of war, 'The irish fighting over God or whats best Protestand or CATHOCIL'. America is wrong, because there they 'assasin all the good important people'. Uncontrolled sex is wrong: premarital intercourse is rarely mentioned, but rape frequently, and such morally diverse sexual practices as adultery, incest, prostitution, abortion and divorce. Even the pill receives a cryptic mention as 'always wrong, unless you know what might happen'. Other predictable offences are cruelty to animals or children, the use and promotion of drugs, colour-prejudice (or indeed *any* prejudice), bullying, gossiping, and blackmail (even 'Playful Blackmailing'). Always wrong, too, are irritating school rules about hair and uniform, corporal punishment, school opening hours ('the time school closes and openes should be later and earlyer'), prison sentences, 'being allowed to drive at about 55 years after taking only one driving test', 'the motorbike age going up'. But wrong too is 'braking the law', or 'going into pubs at less age than now', supporting the IRA, or having a TV without a licence. General wrongs include injustice, such as 'the Poor Beeing separeted from Middle Class top Class', and such personal faults as laziness, greed, selfishness and corruption. Selfishness is both active and passive. It is wrong to 'go about making trouble' and to get others into trouble: 'hurting people for no reason', 'making fun off people', 'using other people for your own wealth', 'to take revenge on someone'. It is equally wrong to be passively selfish: 'not helping anyone', 'not taking notice of other people's points', 'neglecting other people's needs', 'leaving someone out of your friendship'. 'Cheeking adults' is wrong, but so is 'making people do what they don't want to do', and 'teachers picking on certain children'. One despairing child says, 'The world altogether is wrong theres always some sort of war going on.'

From this splendid pot-pourri of moral judgments, received attitudes and private irritations, it is hard to draw any firm outline of the adolescent ideology. And an earnest frequency-count would yield no more startling conclusions than that murder is widely disapproved, and that boo-words like 'laziness' and 'greed' are still boo-words. One or two points do, however, emerge.

First, these children miss the problem of 'always wrong'. The discussion-groups picked it up fairly easily, but it is entirely missed in the written papers. This is perhaps not surprising: a discussion-group is a place where problems emerge as many-sided, a paper-test works by direct association. And the point is, after all, a fairly abstract one. These youngsters are still in advance of the infant school child who defined wrong as 'what teacher says you mustn't', even if they still work in over-simple categories.

Furthermore, it becomes clear that we cannot say this is an unprincipled generation, in the way Coleridge accused young men of being in 1831 (see p. 3). They have no hesitation at all about using 'right' and 'wrong' as if they could be taken to mean something. We might say their confidence is misplaced, that they are only emotive-subjectivists shouting against what they do not like, or that they are sociological-objectivists repeating standard attitudes. But we cannot say that 'no one seems to have any distinct convictions'. All but our female 2% want to say there is something wrong about lying. Some would draw the distinction verbally, and say fibbing or tact is all right; others realize that words are inadequate, and the situations must be examined; but all of them realize that in such doubtful areas there is a principle at work, even if it cannot be stated.

And there is a touch of moral fervour about it all, far removed from the gum-chewing apathy they are said to display: in their tumbling lists of offences, their sense of injustice and compassion, their shrinking from violence and disruption, and their underlying faith in an ordered way of life in which persons may grow.

They do not much like, they say, the notion of a set of commandments that someone else lays down, but they are equipped themselves with a hopeful but not unrealistic set of moral guidelines about which they care. The sheer variety of their list of wrongs may suggest that they have not yet established an agreed order of priorities; but in this they are no worse than their parents. And this same variety also suggests that the conversation, as they carry it forward to adult life, touches a wide moral frontier, within which sensitive living can be amply developed.

2   Mercy-killing

The old

Do you think people with an incurable and painful disease should be put to death?

It's up to the person concerned.

Well, if the person concerned says to the doctor, Look, for heaven's sake, finish me off today?

No, that would be killing people.   A ☐

If he asked the doctor to kill him that would be
committing suicide.   B ☐

But if you want to die you can die. It's up to
you. It's no one else's life. They can't keep you
alive if you want to die.   C ☐

A handicapped baby

If a baby arrives terribly badly handicapped, would you kill it?

They should say to the parents, I can't do anything about it; then the parents can decide.

A baby was born once, and the doctor said, If the mother sees the baby it'll shock her so she'll never be the same again. So he killed it.

And you approve of this?

I don't know.

Would you approve of killing a handicapped baby?   ☐
            disapprove?   ☐
            not know?   ☐

The choices offered here are alike in one respect, but crucially different in another. They both offer a choice between approval and disapproval of mercy-killing, but in one case the victim has some measure of choice while in the other he has none. The distribution of responses is in consequence very different. Two-thirds are ready to accept the right of the old to choose for themselves; only 4% are offended by the notion that there is any choice in the matter at all; and 28% shrink from the deed the killers would have to perform. There are rather more, 38%, to disapprove outright of the killing of babies, only 19% to approve outright, and 43% to confess to the sense of an intolerable dilemma.

RESULTS

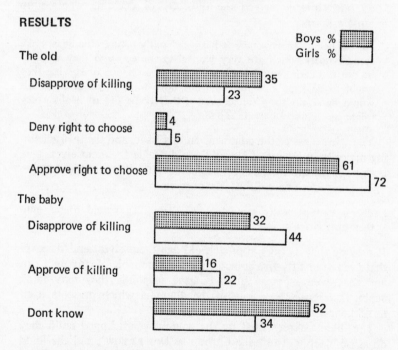

The written comments bring out a further difference, that the problem of the baby comes home to these boys and girls more closely than the problem of old age, to which only 5% of them make any reference. These rare ones usually state their view without seeing the dilemma even in this situation:

It should be up to the people concerned.

No one has the right to take someone else's life, in a way not even the person concerned has, God made us, so we have no right to kill us. That is like trying to be God, *that* is wrong.

Two children had the insight to see that the old might be unable in fact, to choose:

It is up to the person unless they are in no fit state to decide.

I think that when a Person has an uncurable disease, its up to that person to decide if he should be put to death. But again if he's say in a Coma and dosent realise the world about him, and his relitives agree it would be OK.

Only one child perceived the difficulty of deciding what is an *incurable* disease.

An old person or anyone esle has a defenatly incurerable deases like some cancers which are very painful at the end and they want to be put to death should be. But if there is a chance of surving they ought to be kept alive even if they dont want to be because this would be committing suicide and if they come out of it alive they might be thankful they are alive.

The sparseness of the comment on this issue, and the overwhelming majority in favour of letting the old decide for themselves, may both be explained by the sheer remoteness, for them, of the decision to be taken. As one child sagely observed,

People cannot really say which of these they would prefer until they have been in such a situation.

It may be that as they approach old age themselves, and discover that even after fifty-five some of them are capable of driving a car, and that even in pain life may have meaning, they may think again, and sense the agony of the dilemma which presents itself to all concerned.

The dilemma presented by the acutely handicapped child they do sense, deeply. The largest group is 'Don't know'; and the flood of eager comment explores the pain of the situation. As we should expect, girls say more than boys; and perhaps also predictably, more of them have made up their minds: 52% of boys do not know, as against only 34% of girls. Among those who do know, boys and girls emerge equal in the decision they make, a third saying they approve, two-thirds saying they disapprove, of mercy-killing.

They plainly feel themselves close to the problem here, though

some of them realize that the situation cannot be truly felt until
it is real:

> It is easy to say 'Yes, I approve' when I'm writing it on paper. If it
> was my baby or my mother, I probably wouldn't be so sure. If I was
> a mother, whose baby was handicapped, I couldn't say 'yes, you can
> kill my baby'. It's virtually impossible.

> I'm not sure if I approve of killing a handicapped baby, although
> they will never lead a normal life, as they can still be happy, but on
> the other side the child can be a heartbreak to the family. If I was
> the mother in that situation, I couldn't say to the doctor, 'Kill my
> baby'. I don't think any mother could.

The disapproval of killing springs from two kinds of reason:
that killing of any kind is wrong, and that is the end of the matter;
and the difficulty already seen about 'incurable', that we cannot
always be certain that the degree of handicap is sufficient to justify
the denial of life. The first group have things cut and dried:

> I think babys that are born should have a chance to live and see the
> world.

One even sees a possibility of waiting until the child is old enough
to be consulted:

> I'd let the baby have a chance to decide for itself wether or not he
> wanted to be killed off. Let him grow up a bit then see if he's getting
> along alright or if he's fed up with life.

A fiercer clarity appears in those who call it murder: A young
Roman Catholic, for example, says:

> It would be muder to kill the baby as god sent it that way and it
> should stay and have a fare share of the world.

Another child leaves God out of it, but is equally sure of his
ground:

> If a baby is *Handicapped* there is no reason to kill the baby because
> that is *murder*. There reason is that it can be sent to a special school
> and be looked after there is no reason to *murder* it. Because thats
> what it is when the doctor just kills the baby. MURDERING.

Yet another would execute the child-killers:

> Killing a handicapped child is murder in all sences. I think that who
> ever killed a handicapped baby should be killed as well because the
> babies that do have something wrong with them would have a

chance to live. The same as an ordinary person has.

Perhaps showing more insight than these stern moralists are those who see the difficulty of deciding on the degree of handicap, and fear the sheer finality of a decision.

I know a friend who has a handicapped baby – something to do with the spine. When she was born they said that she would never live till the age of six months and she was to be kept in hospital all that time. But the mother insisted that they took her home. They did, and with love and care from all the family she is now seven years old and is able to walk, she is starting at a special school very soon.

'Handicap' and 'normal' are, after all, slippery words:

There is no such word as handicapped. So What there a little difference to us, but they are loved just as much.

And one child, arguing that

Handicaps are not the only things. They may have advantages, a cripple may be a musician,

recalls the grim test-case in this argument, that on an apparently overwhelming set of conditions for the killing of a baby, the decision would have been taken to smother the infant Beethoven.

What of the small but significant number who would approve of mercy-killing? One or two, but only one or two, take a tough-minded, socially-hygienic line that it is necessary for the well-being of the race:

It would be better to kill the baby because if it is mentally handicapped, the government will be wasting its money on it, it will cause a lot of bother and trouble, it will never be able to do things, that ordinary people will be doing, and it won't have a very happy life. Also, if you got rid of these people at birth in time their might be a new generation of people less likely to get dissabilities.

Others appeal to the biology of survival:

As the population grows I think the very badly handicapped baby should be killed. In the animal world the handicapped die. I think man has upset the balance of nature by saving the handicapped. Man kills suffering animals so they should kill suffering babys.

But in general the apparently tough-ones are really motivated by compassion for the child itself, even when, as here, they express themselves in tough language:

I think that if a child of mine was born handicapped and could never lead a normal life I would make *damned sure* I killed it I wouldn't want it to lead the life of a 'cabbage'!

The same point is more tenderly made in,

I think that if the baby were born very handicapped the doctor should just let it die. Because the baby when it grew up (if it grew up) would be just confined to a wheelchair no mind of its own and it would just be a misery. It would be like a zombe.

Perhaps the comment showing most insight comes from a child who sees that love and care can make life significant for even a handicapped child, and makes his decision turn on whether or not that love can be counted on:

I believe in mercy killing, at birth. If a child is severely handicapped, especially if mentally so, the parents should be able to decide on two things. To care for the child, see it gets the proper teaching it needs to develop and live at home. Or to put the child to rest within three days of birth. I am against all forms of institutions where selfish parents can dump children. I think mental homes are appalling for the patients and nurses.

We may feel as we read this that he has not said all that there is to say about any of his conditions; but there is here the ground-work of thought about the problem: compassion and a sense of the agony of the choice, a demand for realism in the examination of the situation, and a demand for courage in making a resolve.

3 *Drugs*

Do you think we ought to make cannabis legal?

No, I say hash and pot and things should be forbidden.

And you don't mind not being able to buy it yourselves?

What would I want to buy it for? We know
what's happened to other people, so why should
we want to buy it?   A ☐

I think taking drugs is all right as long as you
don't try to persuade someone else to take them.   B ☐

What right have the police to stop you taking
drugs?   C ☐

Our boys and girls found this an easy question to answer, and
their views are easy to present. Four-fifths of the girls and three-
fifths of the boys were decidedly against buying drugs for themselves, and only 2% of the girls and 6% of the boys denied the
right of the police to interfere. It is noticeable, however, that the
choices they were asked to make were not mutually exclusive.
It would indeed be possible for somebody to argue that though he
would not take drugs himself, he would deny the right of the state
to prevent others doing so, while being prepared to take a tough
line with peddlers. So here we are asking for an indication of
what it is thought it is most important to say, not a decision on
the over-riding case.

RESULTS

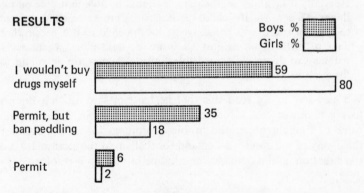

Boys %
Girls %

I wouldn't buy drugs myself — 59 / 80
Permit, but ban peddling — 35 / 18
Permit — 6 / 2

The recoil from the use of drugs is based largely on acceptance
of the remark in the questionnaire, that 'we know what's happened
to other people'.

I have listened to a tape on a girl who took drugs and the results of
it all and I found it really awful. I can't understand how they get
hooked on it in the first place. Many people say there never take
drugs, but most these people do. Something must influence them
to do so.

I think that it is terrible that people should be allowed to take drugs
at all. I would never want to take them, not after all the horrible
things I've heard about it. If more shocking stories, broadcasts,
advertisements and Telivision programmes were shown, what effects
it can have on you I don't think half so many people would be
tempted to take them.

Others have some inkling into why drugs are taken, but still condemn and fear them.

Taking drugs is bloody idiotic! It's a coward's way out if you can't face up to life realistically.

Underlying this recoil is fear and a desire to be protected from corruption. The fear is vague but powerful.

Drugs kill people by driving them mad or making them do things that might endanger other people's lives.

Or, less dramatic but nearer home:

Drugs effect your health and your career. People pass on the street and say nasty remarks to your friends.

And so comes the demand for complete prohibition:

I think drug should be mad Elagal as they kill people or send them potty.

If the could stop all these silly students from taking drugs things would be much better.

Those who opt for permissiveness for takers but not for peddlers are still hostile to the notion of taking drugs themselves.

Taking drugs yourself is OK if your daft enough to. It's your health its up to you to protect it. The police should only intervene when you persuade somebody else to.

If a person chooses to take drugs, it is their decision, but I am against all dope pushers. Personally I would never take drugs because I have seen people, some friends, mentally disturbed to a certain degree, after taking drugs. I would help anyone to break from dope, if I could, if they wanted to. But I think pushers are killers, and I would say these people should be punished. not the people who choose of their own accord to turn to drugs.

Indeed the only defence of drugs comes from a small number who see the point so often made in the debate, that teachers and magistrates utter their fierce denunciations, and then restore their ruffled feelings with tobacco and alcohol.

Drugs are no better or worse than alchocol or smoking. It is not the drugs that are harmful if taken properly and the mild ones are taken, it is the people who push the drugs and persuade small children who know nothing about them that need to be given the chop.

Finally, a very small group shrug their shoulders, and say, Why bother with such people?

> If young people want to kill themselves then let them the world is overpopulated as it is so why bother with them.

> If a person wants to kill themselves by drugs. The let 'em. That's all I can say. Its not really up to me is it.

What emerges from the whole picture is something more encouraging than this: a perfectly proper, though unspecific and ill-informed, fear; a readiness to accept the interference of authority in the protection of children and the immature; and some dim realization that though legislation is difficult, it has some part to play in the maintenance of the health of the community. Nobody talked of drugs as a serious means of exploring hidden frontiers of the personality, or as preliminaries to religious experience; nobody spoke seriously of the issue of personal freedom – the 'why bother?' line of argument is an impatient withdrawal from a complex situation, rather than a positive assertion of drug-taking as a human right.

The last word they are yet ready to utter is perhaps that of a boy who alone sees the problem of law enforcement, and indeed of having laws at all.

> I disagree with drug taking – to me it is pointless, harmful and unnecessary – but if people wish to take it OKay – they should not try to persuade others to join and should not be prosecuted by the police. Surely its only a worsened form of cigarette addiction and is up to the individual concerned. Incidentally if cannabis etc became legal – it would raise the number of takers conciderably whereas being illegal might put some off trying it due to the risk – however once it is illegal – those who break the law must be punished. It's a vicious circle!

4   *A good person*

Like the rest of us, our youngsters are in difficulties over moral rules: how to state them, how to apply them, how authoritative they are, and where their authority comes from. They are in difficulties, too, with trying to describe where they learn them, except for the vague generality 'from your parents' or 'from the home'. They do not know how to think out moral dilemmas, and are in doubt whether there is ever time, in real life, to think them out at all. The actual content of their current moral ideology is not at all unsatisfactory, but the way they acquire it and the way they actually think about it are not at all clear.

The last questions put before them were therefore questions about the moral *person*, seeking to find out what sort of a personal image they conjure up when someone speaks of a good man; and then implicitly but not explicitly connected, what sort of an image do they have of Christians, to see whether the Christian ideal is still operative in the forming of moral attitudes.

What sort of a person would you describe as a 'good person'?

Somebody doing something they were happy doing, that they were good at, not doing something they didn't want to. A ☐

Somebody who tries to change things and make them better, to make less poverty and make it easier for people to live. B ☐

Somebody who has a posh car, nice wife, doesn't drink, doesn't go to Bingo, and you never hear him swear. C ☐

No, that's a goody goody. A good man in my mind is a man who tries everything, and experiments with living and learns by his own mistakes. D ☐

Somebody who can listen sympathetically to somebody else. E ☐

These 'cluster-points' are again not mutually exclusive, as some of the children observed:

I would think a good person was all the things that is statted in B C and E.

(Because I have ticked one doesn't mean I think that is sufficient: all the other definitions contain good qualities)

while one young opportunist produces a breathtaking hold-all view:

Someone who tries to make everything better to himself and the people around him, sombody can listen sympathetically to others, somebody who can be good and helpfull and also learn from mistakes somebody who know to admit his mistakes and know when he was wrong.

But it is still possible to recognize distinct kinds of choice going on here. They may be arranged in a kind of moral continuum, from a somewhat negative conformity to a wide-ranging active concern.

C. Successful conformity. Different social classes would present different elements here, but all classes could produce their own picture of the man who toes the moral line, and obtains his reward. ('There was a man in the land of Uz, whose name was Job; and that man was perfect and upright, and ... his substance was seven thousand sheep and three thousand camels and ...)

A. Individual authenticity: the assertion of the unique self, 'doing your thing'.

D. Individual authenticity that learns about the moral realities of the situation, not from authority, but from personal experience.

E. Sympathetic listening, and the compassionate, supportive personality, more outgoing than the first three, but less active than B. The tender-hearted person who is afraid of being labelled a 'do-gooder'.

B. Active concern for the well-being of others, not just busy in good causes, though he is, but with the inspiration of a view of the good life for human beings to live.

RESULTS

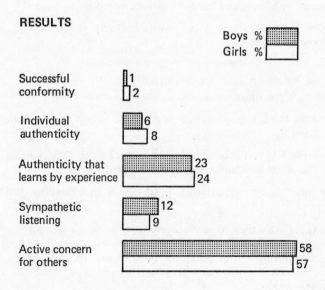

Boys %
Girls %

	Boys	Girls
Successful conformity	1	2
Individual authenticity	6	8
Authenticity that learns by experience	23	24
Sympathetic listening	12	9
Active concern for others	58	57

Boys and girls are here uncannily close together; and they are virtually unanimous (apart from the 1% who get everything wrong) in rejecting from the scene the man with the posh car and nice wife who has risen above the temptations to smoke, swear (at any rate audibly) and play Bingo. This man, our youngsters would say, seems as if he must be dead.

> A person who has a posh car, doesn't drink, etc. is not nesserealay a good person.

> He can swear as much as he likes as long as he don't go around beatting old ladies on the head for their purse.

One boy sees the same point in the light of his own behaviour:

> I'm a good Person even tho I shoot Pigins.

There is not a great deal more support for the individual who does his thing, regardless of consequence, but the point is made, and we should take it, that there is genuine virtue in standing up against pressure to conform:

> I think you should live your own life, do what you want, not what your'e told to do. All through our lives we are given orders from someone. I think people would be far happier doing what they want to do.

> I think a good person is one that sticks to what he thinks without allowing the people around him to influence him.

One boy, whose spelling and grammar put him firmly in the individualist camp, nevertheless sees that 'your own thing' must at some point be judged against 'the right thing':

> I think its all depend what they happy to do, e.g. if they want to kill someone they dont like its what they like to do well it all depend on what, itnt it?

A quarter of them want to think in terms of the authentic individual, living out his own longings, but learning to accept the limitations of reality:

> I personally think that you learn through your own mistakes, and from these mistakes you are able to correct anything which orrcurs again like it.

Here, at any rate, we have the possibility of moral education, conducted by 'discovery' methods, from which there arises a degree of self-control:

> They have learnt to control their own selfish feelings and bad tempers

and from which a wide-ranging set of moral generalizations could be developed.

Fully two-thirds of the responses, however, move away from all this attention to the moral individual, operating from his own nature in a kind of vacuum, and at best learning from experience, over on to the side of 'goodness' as in some fundamental sense a concern with other people. A small number settle for sympathetic listening, a passive, non-interfering attitude:

> Somebody who lets people get on with their own lives and does not stick his/her nose in other peoples business.

> People may be too good and instead of helping you they hinder.

This warning was elaborated by a girl who favours active concern, but sees its dangers:

> A good person has to be happy and unselfish, to help others who need help without being a do-gooder. He needs to understand people and their problems and try to help, to be able to keep his mouth shut when necessary.

But the vast majority agree that passive listening is not enough:

> They should be able to listen to somebody telling their troubles, but not completely sympathetically, putting 2 and 2 together and seeing who's in the right, then say what *you* would do, help them as best you can, but not spoil them to believe they're perfect.

And so, one after another, they develop the argument that goodness is an active virtue, out-going and other-supporting.

> A good person is someone who can love.

And love is a willing thing, not just a feeling thing:

> A good person thinks always of others more than himself, and tries to help people in trouble even if he doesn't like them very much.

But it is a feeling thing as well as a willing thing:

> Someone who is not selfish, but generous to people, not only in money but in affection as well.

So it calls for understanding and sharing in other people's feelings:

> A good person must be able to listen to other people's views even

if he disagrees with them. A Good person must make people around him at rest and happy. Always thinks of other people's feelings before himself.

One endeavours to sum up the whole situation as presented by the choices offered:

A good person is somebody who put themselves out to help uther people, or if they have a problem try to help them as best they can over the problem. People who have posh cars and such like can very often be nasty people, who only think of themselves and money. A good person should be trust worthy and loyal to the people they are trying to help and not discuss their problems with uthers.

And finally a number of comments try to round out the picture of the good person with minor virtues, like gaiety,

He would not be a very serious person, but someone you could have a laugh with,

and humility,

Doesn't try to put on airs and graces,

and cheerful courage,

A person that enjoys almost anything he is doing, and if not, he tries not to show it.

And we are warned of the danger of perfectionism and scrupulousness:

Not neccesarily an angel but a normal being,

and of so categorizing 'good persons' that real people fail to fit in:

Everybody is good in someway.

It is not a bad picture that they carry about with them: a picture of loving, but a genuine loving, springing up from within the personality, stirred by another's need, gay and unassuming, faithful and tender, not standing by uninvolved, not interfering to another's harm.

They are making two fundamental points about the nature of 'goodness'; first, that it arises from an active and serious concern for others; and second, that it is spontaneous and authentic. Put in such general terms, it may appear that nothing much is being said: 'be kind' and 'be sincere' are so unexceptionable as to be almost meaningless, and they simply fall through the gap between the demands of the *ought* and the impulse of the *want*. They fail to notice that the ethical dilemma arises only in a conflict between right and desire. A Boy Scout once said to another, 'Do you ever have days when you feel just a little untrustworthy, disloyal, unhelpful, unfriendly, discourteous, unkind, grumpy, cowardly and irreverent?'

In *Ann Veronica*, H. G. Wells makes one of his characters put the conflict between morality and authenticity as a total choice between one and the other:

> Life is two things, that's how I see it, two things mixed and muddled up together. Life is morality – life is adventure. Adventure rules – and morality looks up the trains in Bradshaw. If morality means anything it means keeping bounds, respecting implications ... If individuality means anything it means breaking bounds – adventure. Will you be moral and your species, or immoral and yourself?

Our young people are not so simple, nor, despite their suspicion of an authoritarian moral code, are they prepared to regard morality as inevitably hostile to the authentic spirit. They overwhelmingly reject the conformist to a narrow code; and almost as overwhelmingly they reject the merely spontaneous character who 'lives his own life, does what he wants, not what he's told to, and sticks to what he thinks without allowing the people around him to influence him.' 'It all depend,' the argument ran, 'on what they happy to do, e.g. if they want to kill someone they dont like its what they like to do well it all depend on what, itnt it?' They insist on the many-sidedness of goodness, 'all the things that is statted in B C and E':

> someone who tries to make everything better to himself and the people around him, somebody can listen sympathetically to others, somebody who can be good and helpfull and also learn from mistakes somebody who know to admit his mistakes and know when he was wrong.

There is implicit here the notion of a man who not only has good impulses, and wants to get his actions *right*, but who can subdue himself to the situation, and learn.

There are, in all this, muddles and false trails, and some plain error; but in the whole picture there is the making of a morality.

4

The Making of a Morality

What do I mean by claiming that there is here the making of a morality? And what kind of a morality is it that is here in the making?

I obviously do not mean that these boys and girls have fully learnt and accepted a prescriptive set of moral rules. Whether they talk about lying or stealing or killing or drug-taking, they decide that the rules will not work. Rules, they even seem to argue, are in themselves immoral, however splendidly they are couched. 'It's something everybody should come to for themselves: it shouldn't be a commandment.' They are here identifying as the moral moment that situation in which the rules are unclear, when they are too blunt or too insensitive to the persons involved or inapplicable to the complexity of the facts. 'You cannot say drug taking is wrong,' they argue, 'until you have made it clear what drug you are talking about, and what kind of harm it does: nicotine and alcohol are drugs, as much as cannabis, and the moral judgment on cannabis, as much as on nicotine and alcohol, turns on quantities and consequences rather than mere names.' The activity of morality is thus for them an activity of judgment, of battling with fact and value, of reconciling contrary compassions, of bending the rule on the fulcrum of the reality of the situation. Moral rules are not like laws, they say, to be stated with authority and clarity; to be looked up in the index and obeyed without question, for looking up and obeying is living at second hand. So if we ask of them, Have they articulated a code of moral prescriptions which will see them safely into their adult life? we should have to say, No, and they have no intention of looking for one.

They have chosen instead to trust themselves to the quick immediacy of personal relationships. Lying may be right, if it is to protect a friend or to avoid hurt feelings, though tact may be wrong if the other person is *counting* on honesty. Be quiet about Aunt

Molly's stupid great big hat, yes, because Aunt Molly would be hurt; but when your mother asks your judgment on her new dress, she wants your judgment, your personal gift of truth. Drug-taking may be right for a person on his own, though wrong if it corrupts another; and even for himself if it changes his identity. Spontaneous behaviour is good, but sympathetic listening is better, because it involves the other. Prudent behaviour, learning from mistakes and improving judgment is good, but not as good as active concern for others. Smothering a handicapped baby offends because the tiny flicker of life counts for something, perhaps enough to outweigh a crippling handicap.

If this were all they had to trust to, we should be terrified for them. They would be at the mercy of the particular personalities among whom, in work and play, they happened to be thrown. When their truth was met by lies, they would give up truth; when their outreaching compassion was rebuffed, they would cease to feel; their trust betrayed, they would cease to trust. Morality, we should want to urge upon them, is not a method of liking people, making friends and being a success: it is a *structure* in which mutual trust develops personal trustworthiness, and makes trusting reasonable; and it must apply to strangers, or it is no more than the cosiness of the in-group, which may itself be an immoral group.

But though these boys and girls state their faith in such personal terms, they also show signs of a generalizing power by which a firmer morality may be developed. They do, after all, *converse.* They are not just shouting in the dark: they are reasoning, listening to each other's arguments and trying to meet them. A morality is, first of all, a conversation, a language of behaviour and relationships. Like a language, it is to some extent given, and it has to be learnt, in an established cultural inheritance. Like a language it has a grammar and a structure. And like a language it can be manipulated by the individual as he develops his own characteristic life-style. These children convey the impression that they have begun to use the language. They have still a good deal to learn about grammar and spelling in the language of behaviour, as they have in the mother tongue; but they can use the language with both understanding and feeling.

Their rejection of rules is not a rejection of the language itself, but an assertion that the mere rules of grammar do not make the language. Their use of the technique of *grading* (lies and fibs, murder and defensive killing, and the rest) is an assertion of the subtlety of the language. Their balancing of the seriousness of the

lie against the seriousness of consequences to the person is an effort
to hold supreme the value of the personal. When they recognize
that small acts of pilfering add up to serious pilfering, they are
generalizing; or that theft from Woolworth's must be judged as theft
from oneself – 'You wouldn't like it' – they are generalizing to
the point of enunciating the Golden Rule. Their claim that even
the Golden Rule is not to be a commandment imposed from above
but 'something everybody should come to themselves' is a claim
that in some way moral laws are 'there' to be arrived at. And the
readiness, in the last analysis, to use the word 'wrong' is a claim
that right and wrong, whatever problems they raise of definition,
have some sort of meaning.

Where has all this come from? How have they learnt it? We
should not want to say, as we follow the twists and turns of their
argument, that they have been explicitly *taught* it. This is not the
talk of the undergraduate ethics class, where rules of procedure are
understood. It shows, indeed, some impatience with rules of procedure, returning obstinately to the personal instance. 'The next
person might be yourself ... If one of my friends stole something
... What would I wanna buy it for? ...'

When we consider the moral situation in which they have hitherto done their learning, we cannot be surprised. They learnt their
first steps in a home where rules were, quite simply, what mother
and father said. The rules were then absolutes, in the sense that
they had to be obeyed, but not in the sense that they had any
existence of themselves. They were not hanging about, as it were,
in the universe, to be called upon and consulted. If parents were
reasonably consistent in what they said, then their sayings would
develop habits of behaviour, with characteristics similar to obedience to rule. But they were not obedience to rule: they were
obedience to persons. And in practice, parents can never be entirely consistent. They have their off days, when what is normally
tolerated becomes intolerable; their good days, when what is
normally risky becomes possible. Reading the book of morals, for
a young child, is thus little more than reading the message of a
human face.

It is much the same for the first few years at school. One teacher
steps into the role of a five-hour mother, and lays down the law
in much the same absolute but inconsistent way. The rules may
now be more regularly enforced, but they still vary so much from
moment to moment that it is not safe to follow them without keeping in touch with the teacher as a person. It is safe to wander about

and talk while you are doing your 'research'; not so safe while teacher is reading a story. And some things are safe on a sunny Tuesday morning that become perilous on a wet Friday afternoon.

For most of the time during the first ten years of life there is a sense of being personally watched. 'God', it used to be said, 'has his eye on you.' The child would agree that this is so, and he responds, sometimes anxiously, sometimes confidently, by keeping his eye on God. His only possibilities of exploring the moral situation, and testing out a general moral principle, is to imitate his parents or, less easily, his teacher, and discover whether or not what applies to them can be made to apply to him. A small boy, reproved by his mother for swearing, argued that 'Daddy says it.' 'But Daddy's Daddy,' said his mother. 'Well, I'm I'm,' he replied. But in this effort at generalization, his opportunities are limited; and probably, if we could know, not very desirable. Adult life looks, after all, rather boring, and not worth imitating.

Where he does imitate, however, as when he is practising a skill under his teacher's guidance, he begins to encounter the word 'wrong', when he fails, and 'right' when he succeeds. The word is not meant to have a moral connotation here, but it is uttered in various tones of approval and disapproval, and carries much the same message as if it *were* moral: the message that something has been done so as to win reward or punishment. He has a long way to go, in both conduct and arithmetic, before he can reach the stage of relying on his own insight, and know he is right whether he is approved or not.

Before that stage can be reached, he has had the extra confusion of discovering that approval and disapproval can also be conveyed by his peers, as they begin, slowly but powerfully, to count towards his self-esteem. They are confusing, because they approve and disapprove of different things, they are not consistent with themselves, and they give even less explanation of the reasons for their judgments. So he is still not discovering a rule-system: he is simply increasing and diversifying his rulers. He is still obeying, or disobeying, persons. If the pressures are too conflicting he will be not merely confused about how he ought to be, but confused about who he is himself, and become uncertain about his own identity.

But it is from his own sense of identity that he forges his sense of justice: 'I'm I'm' cannot be said by a child who is doubtful about 'I'm'. We cannot, after all, put ourselves in someone else's shoes unless we have a self to put.

What I am arguing here is that the young adolescent, as he moves into the period when home begins to count for less, and the peer-group begins to count for more, operates on a morality of personal relations, created and sustained largely in face-to-face situations by people he can actually see; and he has little opportunity of doing much more. If he is to have any sort of grasp of a more generalized mode of moral thought, he will have in some way to be taught it. It is for this reason that the concept of moral education has recently received a good deal of attention; and it is for this reason that we must now ask what our boys and girls think they have received in this area, and what they make of it. The two chapters that follow try to answer this question.

5

Talking about Moral Education

1 The role of the school

It would be easy to get children to talk about their education in any school subject other than the 'subject' of morality. Children and their teachers know what mathematics is, and they know what would count as success in it. But we are none of us clear what morality is, and could not agree on what counts as success. Is an obedient child more or less moral than a disobedient child? Well, we might say at first, more. But what if it is Fagin that he obeys? Here four groups try to identify the moral purpose of the school, and say what notion of goodness is held up before them.

(i) What kind of person would this school, as you have known it, be considering 'good'? What sort of qualities of a human being do you think they are encouraging?

> I think to go on studying after you've finished school. They like you to do this a lot, I think. And to get a decent job and do more studying.

> Your behaviour, in lessons and round school, you know, your behaving well.

What would you think they think 'behaving well' is?

> Doing what they ask you.

> Yes, to respect people, I think.

Do you think 'doing what you're asked' is what they want you to do when you grow up? There's a difference here, isn't there, between being a 'good pupil' at school and being a 'good person' later on? If they are concerned about making you do what you are told now, well fair enough, but do you think this is what they want you to do after you leave?

Yes, for a certain time – at work – till your mind's grown and you've got some ideas. Teachers sort of run you round and get you to get on with your own work.

Now what about later on in life? Do you think this is a great virtue?

It's not a virtue. It's something that you need, really, because sometimes you're going to be dependent on yourself, and if they're going to train you at school you're going to get on better.

It helps you to get on with people, and you do need sometime to be on your own more.

I think they put the pressure in a good way because it *is* left to you what you do as far as work is concerned, and if you don't get it in then they sort of hint that you should have got it in but there's no real pressure that you're going to get a detention or anything like that and I think it helps you to learn to decide for yourself, make your own decisions.

(ii) What kind of qualities do you think the school is trying to promote?

A hard-working person who tries hard.

To be religious in some way.

What would you mean by that?

Your standards to be linked with religion. Not like you go to church every Sunday, but if you do, you know it's somewhere in your background.

What sort of difference is there between being religious and not religious? What sort of things have you in mind?

Well, you're supposed to say prayers and that. Things like that. They talk about that quite a bit.

Well, we'll come back to this in a moment. Any other things you'd like to say about what the school is trying to promote?

Making a place in society, and if you don't want to make a place in society, well, hard luck, but you've still got to.

Yes, they seem to think we've got to be brainy and have a top position in some firm or other and earn a lot of money and have a good life.

There's another reason, of course, they want you to stay on at school. I mean if you're somebody in the bottom set they don't particularly bother about you; if you're somebody brainy you're all right and they try to promote your ideas and all that and get you to do what they want and then you'll probably stay on to the sixth.

Well now, what's wrong with this? Don't you like it?

No, it's up to us what we're going to do. Perhaps we have got brains some of us, but we can still be happy, can't we? A person can still be happy doing nothing.

It's better to be poor and happy than rich and sad.

There's a lot of hippies, they're brainy, but they choose to walk the streets and do what they like. They're happy.

Most hippies are making a protest against everyday society because they don't agree with it and they're making a stand. They may change society one day.

You seem to be saying that the school is pushing you in a direction you don't want to go in. Where does it do the pushing?

The careers room, and everywhere. They say, Carry on with hard work in your job and keep quiet and don't bother anybody.

Yes, and where's that going to get you? Nowhere, is it?

What's your alternative here? Do you object to working hard?

No, I've no objections to working hard. It's when the teacher sets you something that you know ... you have a choice of lessons, before we didn't have a choice of lessons, there was something we detested, and we did work we knew we were going to give up afterwards ... never taught us anything, because we just weren't interested, you just didn't bother about it.

Why do you think they do this?

Well, it's to tell you what you want to know. You don't do physics and chemistry in the junior school, and if you had to choose when you were eleven you wouldn't know what you were about.

If you look at the school and ask yourself the question, Now what kind of a person do they think is a good person? What are they trying to do to me? what would you say?

Someone who does well in social life and doesn't drink too much, doesn't smoke.

Yes, but that's all out of school time – social life, half of that's in school time, but smoking and drinking – most of that's in your own time.

But do you think the school is still interested in it?

> Yes. They're interested in your living a normal life, getting you qualifications to do the jobs.

> When you're smoking outside the school and a teacher catches you and it's in your own home, they want to know about it directly you get into school. And really it's none of their business. But they say, 'You come from Blank Street School', and they don't want you to give it a bad name. I think they're mainly thinking of the school more than when we've left.

Do you agree about that?

> Well, I think what we do is our own affair. *We* suffer from what we do.

> Well. I'm sure that they *mean* well, to try and stop us. There's no complaint about it, but I wish – I mean – ...

> Poverty starts at school, because once you get to the fourth year, if you take academic subjects then teachers start to push you into better jobs, but if you don't then they sort of leave you alone more and gradually the pressure gets less and less for you to try hard.

Are you suggesting that the school would disagree with your view that the good man is somebody who works for change, against poverty and so on?

> But they don't approve of people going on strike for what they believe in. But if a good person wants to change conditions he's got to go on strike.

> Yes, but teachers went on strike, didn't they?

> Trouble is, the teachers in this school have so many different ideas, really.

I believe that at this school, you have a course of instruction on 'The Art of Living'. Do you think you are any *better* now at the art of living than you were when you came to the school?

> We've only had two lessons: we've only done 'the art of living' this term.

> Yes, but that's not the question. He asked us whether we're better or not at getting on with people. I mean 'the art of living' isn't really necessary for getting on with people, is it?

> Well, that's what it's supposed to teach us.

> Well, I think it's wrong then, that idea.

Yes it is, because you're *born* to get on with people. You know whether you can get on with people when you speak to them. They can't change something inside of you to make you get on with people. You can be a friendly sort of person but school lessons can't change you like that.

Well then, do you think you are better at this than when you came at eleven?

Yes, because we've met more people.

People with different ideas – you see how people think.

We've got our own viewpoints now. We've learnt quite a bit about the world since eleven. I mean we know quite a lot more than we did when we were eleven. And we've got our own viewpoints on most things – well practically everything.

When you were eleven you just took what teacher said for granted, now you argue it.

Do you think you are 'five years better' now than when you came to this school?

Yes, I think so ... well ...

Well, yes, I'd hope that is the answer. Now in what sort of way – being perfectly honest with yourself, and not bragging to anybody and not being modest – in what ways would you say you had actually become better in these five years?

Mentally.

Meaning?

Well, you've advanced your knowledge.

I think when you were a bit younger, you didn't care so much about your manners, but when you get a bit older you respect your parents more, I think, and you respect your parents' friends, and your manners ...

I think this doesn't come from school but from your family, your family background.

I don't think the school makes you a better man. It just stops you going downwards.

I think the best thing about school socially is it helps you to mix with everybody.

(iii) Looking round yourselves as a group, would you say you were 'better' in terms of being a good person than you were four years ago, when you came to this school?

> We've matured a bit.

What would you mean by that?

> We don't prance around giggling, and dance around the playground, do we?

> When you see the first years now you sort of think, Aren't they childish?

(iv) Do you in any way feel school has affected your personality or your ideas about goodness or badness?

> Well, I think school's bound to affect your relationship with other people. But I think primary schools don't give children enough responsibility in an individual trust in each other, and they're told what to do, they're expected to do it; and then they get to secondary school and they're suddenly expected to behave well. The difference between the two is far too great.

Would you think that is entirely the primary school's fault?

> It's not entirely either. It's just that there's too big a gap between them. There should be more of a link.

> I think it's very difficult for the primary school teachers, though, because, say, you get some children who come to the primary school at the age of five; and some are very trustworthy and some are very capable. And the others probably, you know, come from a large family of children and probably the teachers won't be able to do anything with them. And they *have* to be ordered around, so they get used to it. What do they do then?

I agree there's a problem. But let's get back to your situation as secondary school people. Tell me about the effect your school has had on you.

> For a start, anyway, I think girls' schools aren't a good idea at all, because of all the cattiness of girls. (*laughter and protests*)

> In the first year you used to go around saying, I hate that so-and-so. But now your outlook's broadened and you don't actually feel as though you hate anybody. You just dislike them.

You've become more tolerant?

> (*Voices*) Yes ... yes ... yes.

> Yes, you just keep out of their way if you don't like them. You

just don't want to have anything to do with them. Well, I mean, as far as possible.

To a great extent I think that this is because you're growing older anyway. You're getting more used to people, you're more out in the world, you're on your own more. So it's not school, really.

2   *Conflict between home and school*

A certain amount of tension between life at home and life at school is inevitable and desirable. At worst, it is a preparation for tension between home and work; at best it offers a wider range of personal options and a richer sense of identity. But we should want our children to move between the two without feeling that they live double lives, in two conflicting climates. Do they really feel this to be so?

(i) Somebody mentioned conscience just now. Where do you get your conscience from? Where does anybody get it from?

Somebody sets you standards.

Who?

Your parents.

Where do they get their standards from?

Do you sense any disagreement between what you would call your conscience, which you say you get from your parents, and the *school's* picture of being good?

They both don't want you to do what you want to do. If you want to smoke, you're not allowed to smoke at school and you're not allowed to smoke at home. There's things like that you're not allowed to do at school or in the house, but you do otherwise.

So your impression is that the school and the home are more or less ganging up together on this?

They're trying to do what they think best, but they don't give people a chance to say what's best.

Well, but do they broadly agree on what's best?

Some parents do. If they've got O levels and A levels they agree more than those that haven't.

No, I don't agree. If parents are more intelligent, they can see more flaws in their arguments.

Do you think that is in fact so? Obviously it could be so, but could you honestly say that it is?

> Yes, your parents have been through exactly the same treatment as you've been through and they can see what it leads to.

So you think they broadly approve of school ethics?

> But it's getting less and less of a straight and narrow way. When schools first started, if you didn't learn your work you were whipped and things like that and it's growing gradually better, so in a few years time, when we're grown up and might be teachers, it'll be better then, but children will still disagree with us.

(ii) Do you think there is any area, in this business of right and wrong, where school and home are disagreed? Would you say that home and school are broadly agreed on – shall we say – what a good person is?

> Broadly, yes ... yes.

> Well, it depends on the family, doesn't it? If you've got a family where there's bad manners and no respect, then the school's going to teach them differently.

> I think if people are brought up in a situation where they're not respectful, then they tend to see things as they are, but if they're respectful to everyone then they get servile to everyone, I think – like Japanese people.

By 'respect' here you're meaning kow-towing, are you?

> Well, not to that extent – but just believing what everybody says.

> Yes, when 'respect' means not to question anything. You disagree about something and your mother says you've to be respectful about something, and she means you're not to question anything.

> I don't think the school teaches you good manners, or respect. I think you come to school with a certain amount in you.

> No, I think it just stops you doing anything bad. I don't think it tells you you're going to be good – it just says you're not going to be bad.

> There's too many people to cultivate manners. You have to leave that to parents.

What are you meaning by manners here? Do you mean being polite in a conventional sense? In terms of manners, you've been perfectly mannered round the table this morning. I would say that listening to each other and taking each other's points seriously *is* good manners. Actually listening to people, isn't this what goes on in school?

Yes, yes.

It might not be so. You could imagine a school in which you never learnt this because you never talked to each other at all – where teachers were teaching all the time and you were writing notes, and you weren't allowed to talk in the corridors, with no situations like this, just talking round a table. I would have thought this was a way in which this school is actually promoting something.

Yes, yes.

(iii) Would you say that the school and parents are on the whole agreed about this? Do you see the school as something which is carrying out the parents' wishes?

Well, parents are different. Some parents let their children smoke, and other parents don't. You can't say 'All parents'.

But would you feel that when you're at home there's a whole different set of values from the values at school?

Oh yes, yes ...

In what way?

Well, at school teachers are strangers really. When you come to school you'd like to try anything on them, but with your father and mother, they're your own flesh and blood and therefore you wouldn't cheat them so much.

If you're still at home and they agree, you can smoke indoors. Yet if you come to school and you ask the teacher, right, can I have a cigarette or something, he'd send you straight to the headmaster. I reckon if your parents agreed you could smoke now and again then I reckon you should smoke at school.

Yes, in a special space – some rooms or something. And have a smoke then. But you must have a letter from your parents agreeing you can do this.

3   *Punishment*

Moral control, we should want to say, is at best positive, working by a vision of goodness, and an inward, voluntary response to the vision. 'Whatsoever things are true, honest, just, pure, lovely, of good report, think on these things.' But moral control has its negative side. The good man, our children say, learns by his mistakes.

Parents and teachers have to see that mistakes are learnt from; and they sometimes impose penalties, to bring home that mistakes are mistakes, that lead to painful consequences. We should expect children not to *like* punishment: they are not meant to. But do they see the moral point it tries to make? Do they learn from it? Three groups discuss the matter.

(i) The thing I think teachers don't remember, when they give you punishments ... well, *they* were probably worse ... My dad keeps on reminding me, he says, Oh, you shouldn't do this and that and yet he tells me stories about how bad he was at school and all the things he did at school – they don't remember this when they give you a good hiding or hit you round the ear-'ole.

Do you think punishing does actually have an effect on people's conscience?

Yes a great effect – it makes you go even further than you meant.

Would this apply to all punishment?

Yes. If they have a quiet chat with you and tell you not to do something the chances are you won't do it. If they threaten you or say you'll stay in a month if I find you doing that again, it makes you more stubborn. It's the same at school, because if the teacher shows you up before the whole class and says it's awful or something like that, then you'd think, Oh, blow 'er, I shall keep on talking. If she asks you nicely after the lesson to be a bit more quiet, you might.

(ii) Would you think punishments are *useful*, assuming they are broadly deserved?

Yes, I think you've got to have them.

What would they be useful for?

Well, they teach us to learn respect for the teachers.

But it's teaching people to bow down, isn't it? I mean, if you hit them hard enough they're going to be respectful to you, aren't they?

I think that if somebody gets the cane or detention it's just ineffective.

It doesn't help you in the long run, anyway.

Why not, do you think?

Well, if you keep having it it doesn't mean anything.

If people are so stupid that they won't accept anything then you might as well throw them out of school. But if they're prepared to listen to why they're wrong then you just tell them.

But if you throw them out of school you're punishing them, and you just said you were against punishment.

No, I just want to send them to another school. I'm against hitting people – that's different.

So am I – but you're still believing in punishment, aren't you?

We might leave the actual mechanics out – hitting or something else. The question is, if somebody does something against the rules, is it a good thing for him that you then impose some painful experience?

I think what does more good than caning them or just slippering them is to sit them down and give them a stern talking to and get them to understand what they're doing.

Yes, if you respect your teacher you won't try to do the things you would get punished for.

But are you more likely to respect a teacher if he punishes you?

You'll dislike him.

It depends on the punishment. If the pupil thinks the punishment's unfair it's going to be worse for his respect.

It all depends if it's something humiliating then you'll *think* he's wrong no matter whether you were wrong or not.

I got into trouble once and the headmaster he didn't give me any punishment at all, he just talked to me. And I found it's a lot better and I respected him more and I still like him. P'raps if he'd punished me I might not have liked him so much now.

Then when you hate the teacher you go to the other extreme: because if you don't like them you're not going to listen to their lessons or work so hard.

(iii) Do you think you learn anything from punishment?

Well, if you get punished I think it makes you more reluctant to work. Like when you get a report saying 'Work! You *must* work,' you think, '*I'm* not going to work. Why should I? Why should *they* rule my life?' But if you realize, in your *own* mind, that you must work, to get a good job and everything, for your parents' sake, you *do* work. Better than being punished.

If a person's getting punished, then he's only going to get more angry, won't he? Then continue not doing work.

Yes, he'll bear a grudge.

You've got to find out the reason why they're not doing work. Sometimes it's laziness but it could be something at home they're brooding about.

What about punishment in the adult world? If someone drives a car dangerously slap through the town, would you punish him or not?

Well, he's an adult – he's matured. And he really ought to know why he did that.

What's the difference? If there's somebody in the second form who doesn't work, you'd say *he* ought to know.

Well, you see, he's not matured, is he? He's only a child and he's just tasting the mistakes you do in life. A lot of people have made a lot of mistakes. And I think they learn by it.

Would you be in favour of running a school without punishment?

No, I think you should have some punishments. If you had no punishments at all then it would just be a wild madhouse.

4 *Religious education*

Until the last few years, it was assumed that the prime vehicle of moral education was religious studies. Here, it was argued, was the supreme source of man's longing for goodness; here, and here alone, the vision of perfection. Four groups examine the question, and though they see a little, and love a little, of the vision, they suspect it may actually do more harm than good.

(i) Does the religious education you get in school affect your attitude to right and wrong?

(*Voices*) No.

Why?

We are split up now, and we have 'Personal Relationships' for half the time and the other half is RE. At the moment I'm having RE and I'm so bored I don't listen for half the time. I just stare out of the window and wish for the time to go by. And she reads out of the Bible for hours.

You feel this is not to do with you?

> No, it doesn't interest me a tiny bit. And if she'd talk about something actually dealing with our lives, you know, about religion and things ...

So you would say it has no effect?

> Not this kind of RE.

Do you think Christianity as an institution has an effect on your lives? I mean, not necessarily as you have it in school but in society at large?

> Um, it puts me in a dilemma. I'd just prefer it if it wasn't there, quite honestly. Because it really confuses me. I'd prefer Christianity not to be there whatsoever.

Could you explain? *I'm* a bit confused.

> Not to exist. I wish it had never been started. Or that I had been brought up to be a strict Christian. One extreme or the other. But at the moment I just don't know.

You have the dilemma of knowing of its existence but doubting its truth?

> Yes.

> But does she realize that if it wasn't for Christianity she wouldn't be here now? All those wars that went by ... If it wasn't for Christianity half the brutality wouldn't have stopped.

(*Voices of protest*) Christians *started* much of the brutality.

> Well, our society has been built up by Christian rules, because if we go back to Hebrew times you can draw almost parallels. I was doing my friend's homework for her once, and she had all these notes. I was quite surprised. You know. About all the parallels that could be drawn between the two different societies.

Would you say that the basic ideas in Christianity are ideas of which you would approve?

> M'm.

I mean, let us say that we are not necessarily believers, but the idea of loving thy neighbour ...

> (*Voices*) Yes ... M'm ...

There are so many people.

> Loving thy neighbour, it's lovely that you should strive for it,

it's very nice, very good sort of thing. But it's very difficult. I think it's rather difficult for people to relate it to themselves, because it's so good.

But at least you can try.

It's good to have something to strive for.

I think it makes it easy to get so discouraged. I know I do. I'm so wicked (*with a chuckle*) I mean, I'll never get any better.

There are so many people in society today that think of themselves as Christians, they go round and say they're Christians. But how many people actually do Christian things? I mean, they don't *do* anything.

So you'd say there's not much distinction between the actual behaviour – as opposed to the beliefs – of a Christian and a non-Christian?

Not really, no.

Not now, years ago they did.

What *are* Christian things? What do you call a Christian?

A Christian is somebody that, um, trusts people, and how many people nowadays trust people?

But there are some people ...

Oh there are *some* people, yes. But there are *lots* who call themselves Christians, and they are Christians, but they don't act like it.

How do you know they are Christians if they don't behave like it?

Because they just accept that they are.

But you can't accept that you are a Christian if you *say* you're a Christian, if you believe, but don't *do* it. You can't say you are.

If you were asked what your religion was, what would *you* say?

I'd say I was a Christian.

Right. Do you go round helping old ladies across the road?

That's not being a Christian.

To live happily and to get on with people you must behave in a Christian way. You needn't necessarily believe in the Christian teaching.

What would you say *is* a Christian way?

Well, the Bible states that God is love. If you love everybody else as you love yourself – this doesn't mean you've got to think they're all perfect, because you know you're not perfect yourself. You dislike yourself. You dislike your enemy. You're supposed to love your enemy – you can still dislike them as well. God is love and you've got to try and love everyone else and treat them as you would treat yourself in that situation. And this is the basis of all Christianity.

And this is a good basis, you would think, for life?

(*Voices*) Yes ... yes ...

(ii) Would you think that the sort of picture you've got of religion has anything to do with right and wrong? Is a good Christian different from a good man?

Yes, conscience. Everybody has a conscience.

Yes, somebody who's a firm believer in God takes some money – he'll have it more on his conscience than somebody who doesn't believe in God and just goes and takes it.

Do you think this is really so? Why?

Because they believe in God, because they believe in their sense. And the rules and standards they set down.

A good Christian isn't the same as a good person because they follow the Ten Commandments and then they look down on anybody else, look down their noses at them.

I think a good person who isn't a Christian is a better person because a Christian does something wrong and he knows it is wrong. Well, he can blame himself because he knows it's wrong, but somebody who doesn't know about being a Christian doesn't know any better.

You're not at the moment saying he's a better or worse *person*. You're only saying that he doesn't feel so troubled afterwards.

The Christian, soon as they do something wrong, they think that they're forgiven for it, by God, so they think that whatever they do wrong they're forgiven. While anybody who doesn't believe in God doesn't care, so he's not worrying about what God thinks of him.

I'm not clear about what you are saying. Are you saying that the person who doesn't believe in God has more conscience or less than the non-believer?

Same. He has just as much conscience, if not more.

Where does he get it from?

> Well, God's just the same as a ghost or a fairy, or something like that, that you believe in. Everybody has some fancy that they believe in. It's just that there's more people believe in God than anything else.

Do you think that's really so?

> We haven't got any proof, have we, that the Bible wasn't just a book made up?

> Like a comic or something like that. Because it could have been written by anybody. Things like Noah's Ark – nobody's got any proof of things like that, not really proved. They may be part of an art lesson, but nobody can say they really happened.

But would you say a Christian would have a conscience, independently of anything he reads in the Bible?

> Yes, because everybody, Christians and non-Christians, everybody's got a conscience. But you can't say that a Christian's conscience is stronger than anybody else's.

(iii) When you think about whether the school has helped you to grow up as 'better' people, would you say that religious education has had anything to do with it?

> (*Voices*) No ... no ...

> Not in the first part of the school – it's just Bible stories and things about the Bible which don't do anything.

What about school prayers?

> I think it helps.

> (*Voices*) I don't ... I don't ... I don't.

> The school shouldn't push you into wanting to be religious an' that, you've got to decide for yourself, on your own experience.

What the school would answer here, presumably, is that they want to help you to decide for yourself, but that before you decide you need to know something about it. Right?

> Yes, that's where the school would help you, because a lot of people wouldn't get religious education at home and they wouldn't go to church so the school would be the place to learn.

(iv) No, I don't think you should have religious education, nor the assemblies so much. A lot of youngsters I know now don't believe in God, and when we have RE there's always the question popping up, you know, Do you believe in him and that, and of course there's a big argument and that and of course it goes right through the lesson. Personally I don't believe in him myself.

But do you think there's any harm in discussing this?

No, I don't mind discussing things. But if a person's got his belief then let him believe in it. I haven't got my belief.

But does the school help you to think it out for yourselves?

I think they've got that idea, but it's not happening at all. I'm not interested in RE you know. I'm just wanting to learn maths and English and all that to help me in my future. I mean, if a bloke wants to be a teacher of religious education, then let him be that. I'm not interested in it.

I don't mind discussing it. It's the other people. If they start criticizing themselves for swearing and that ... I like a good discussion if it's sensible and that.

Do you sense any pressure in religious education towards being a good person?

One thing they do is read a part of the Bible and then try to form you into that person they're talking about.

6

Thinking about Moral Education

1 *The role of the school*

The school's role in moral education might be broadly defined as

1. Guarding children against corrupt pressures while they are still too young to cope with them.
2. Providing experience of personal relationships in a healthy group life conducted under a measure of adult control.
3. Presenting moral knowledge, and practice in moral thinking.

Our boys and girls were asked which of these they saw as most important.

Some boys and girls of fifteen were asked if they thought they were better now than when they came to their secondary school at eleven. They all thought they were. So then they were asked if this improvement was due to the influence of school.

I don't think the school makes you a better man: it just stops you going downwards. A ☐

I think the best thing about school socially is it helps you to mix with everybody. B ☐

We know a lot more than we did when we were eleven, and we've got our view-points on most things. When we were eleven we just took what teacher said for granted, now we argue it. C ☐

There are few to say that the school does no more than prevent them going down – and the few are nearly all girls, the unclubbable sex for whom intimate relationships are more important than social ones. *Per contra*, there are more boys to rejoice in the knowledge and skill that gives them a view-point of their own, and the ability to argue it.

RESULTS

The school

Boys %
Girls %

Just stops you going down

1
14

Helps you to mix

31
34

Helps you to your own view-points

68
51

In the comments, a few say that school did nothing for them at all.

It has not helped me as I have learnt nothing well I suppose you couldn't say I hadn't learned enything it just that after a while you are at school you get fed up off it.

School has made me miserabell and I'll be glad when I see the back of it.

Others see little difference in themselves since they were eleven, and look back to the junior years as most significant for growth:

No I haven't I have learnt all this in my Junior School

though some would not agree, at least about the change in their friends:

I find that a lot of people at junior school have turned completely different since they have come to this school. I think this happens at any secondary school.

And others say, sensibly enough, 'in some ways yes, in some ways no':

In some ways, for now we can argue with them. In some way it hasn't for the tend to nage about small things to much.

Some, though showing no hostility to school, maintain that any change in their personality would have happened in any case:

You grow-up anyhow, eventally.

while others argue that the school cannot hope to reach the personal depths:

Not really. Because a person's a person their character destines if they're going to be good or bad, also the kind of life they live at home. In a way school has helped, helped me to understand better, I think, that's about it.

Among the many recognitions of the influence of school on personal development, the two main themes are the ones offered as choices: socialization and individual development. 'Mixing with people without being shy', 'helping to make friends and to be a good member of the community', learning not to be 'shy to talk to the boys', not merely as social skills but as experience that affects the underlying attitudes:

> It has taught me to get on with people around me I was always selfish I think now that I've grown out of it, and being at school has taught me to accept things I never thought I would.

Though some are not so sure that social experience *does* reach very deep:

> I don't know. I'm not sure if it was school that helped me, or if I would have improved anyway. I'm more mature, but that's no thanks to school. I mean at school you muck about and school doesn't encourage you to mature. School has helped me socially though. I mean once I would never have sat next to a boy at school, but now, after some time, I can sit without embaressment.

This kind of learning, it is very sensibly observed, is more directly received from the peer-group than from teachers – and none the worse for that. It could, after all, be argued that the main task of the school in moral education is simply to bring together boys and girls in favourable circumstances and then let them do the job for each other: it is what adults have to do for each other. And so, say some, what matters is not due to the school:

> Not the school, the pupils, all growing up all wanting to know things, curious. We couldn't have asked the teachers or our parents they would have thought our questions repulsive. So we turned to each other – we were all in the same boat so we had nothing to be shy of.

The other main theme is that of learning to argue 'for oneself'.

> I was very shy but having someone wanting to hear my oppinions cured that (I got sat on a alot at my primary school) I find things out for myself more than before. I think about what teachers say instead of just absorbing it like a sponge to churn it out again word for word at examinations.

> It has helped you to develop a personality and opinion because you are constantly up against opposition in everything, at school you can

discuss and air your opinions on different things. Some teachers are OK to talk to, but there are still the stiff ones who believe kids have no minds of their own and have to be told what to do. These teachers ruin school and the relationships between teacher and pupil.

These two would want to say that the social scene is necessary, but the object of it is not mere adjustment or accommodation but the discovery in argument of personal identity. So, more emphatically, does this one:

> You have mixed with many people so you have got used to how to get on with the different types of people. We have built up to stick up for what we belife.

Another reconciliation between accommodation and individuality is offered by a child who sees the process of personal learning conducted by means of and for the purpose of entering into other people's lives:

> It has given me more knoledge and taught me how to find things myself and helped me to mix more with people and make friends with them

while some realize that they owe to their school learning a capacity for general compassion:

> I have learned more about life in other countrys and the poverty in these countrys.

Teachers would be the first to accept as a fact of life that some of the most important learning goes on outside school. School, they would want to say, is in the end concerned with how to learn rather than with what to learn: the educated man is not primarily marked by his sheer knowledge but by his capacity to find his way about the world. So they would be happy with the comment that

> I know more about history, geography, RE ect. that is facts and figures – thanks to school. But I think I learn more about the 'ways of the world' from my parents, television, and other influences

though they might feel something has gone wrong for the child who writes, sadly,

> I realise more of what goes on in the world now than I did before, therefore I am less happy.

2 *Conflict between home and school*

There is an early limit to what we can ask children about their debt to their home. Home is still in a large measure the form of the self, so the question is too tender to put. Homes are infinitely various, so the answers would be unmanageably divergent. The question that was put, 'Do school and home *differ*?' is not forbiddingly painful, and is capable of some generalization. In the event, the children answered it cheerfully enough, and on the whole reassuringly.

Do you find that the school and your parents often differ about what is right and wrong?

No, they both don't want you to do what you want to do.	A ☐
They're trying to do what they think's best, but they don't give people a chance to say what's best.	B ☐
Sometimes. If parents have got O levels and A levels they agree more than those that haven't.	C ☐
It depends on the family, doesn't it? If you've got a family where there's bad manners and no respect, then the school's going to teach them differently.	D ☐

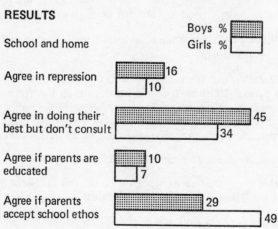

RESULTS

School and home — Boys % (shaded) / Girls % (open)

Agree in repression — 16 / 10

Agree in doing their best but don't consult — 45 / 34

Agree if parents are educated — 10 / 7

Agree if parents accept school ethos — 29 / 49

One child registered his disapproval of the question, and warned us off this delicate area:

> None of you Bisness.

Some few were conscious of conflict, to the point of some pain:

> If you have a working class background then you are at a great disadvantage.

But for the most part all they notice is the distinction inevitable in places that set out with different tasks. Home is, rightly, a cosier and, within limits, a more permissive place than school. School is, rightly, a cooler place, in which relatively impersonal roles are played, and in which pressures are applied to persuade people to act in ways they would not, without such pressure, have thought of acting for themselves. So some children see that there is a distinction, but do not feel themselves forced into a choice:

> I'm not sure as they bothe agree on some and not on other.

Some sense the difference between a place for learning and a place for living:

> The school just want you too take O levels and A levels and don't want you to do what you realy want.

Others sense a lack of enthusiasm at home for A levels and for the academic world, with parents fearful lest their child will become a stranger:

> The school thinks I'm supposet to be a goody goody but my parents want me to have a good job but not be a queer brainy-boy.

School rules come in for some mild attack, usually directed towards the inevitable uniform:

> I do think that my home and my school differ, they differ on many things, School Uniform for one, once your in the forth year you could wear a diffent coat, any coat you want to But my School thinks not, and also the length of boys hair they should not be aloud the hair below the top of the shirt collar so the school say.

Others sense the difference in emotional tone:

> My father cares a lot about what I become. But at school they don't really care. There are a few who do. But the majority don't.

Or, more temperately and, we might say, more realistically,

In some ways they do differ. This is a difficult question. But they do want (my parents) me to get on and get a good job with promise and a job I'll enjoy doing. Also teachers teach you, *but* they don't care so much, (they don't get involved, not that I blame them) but they agree I should get a job I enjoy and have a chance in.

The difference is not always seen as one in which home is to be preferred:

Sometimes I feel better at school as I enjoy the company of other people and the work we do at school but sometimes when I get home I feel depressed and bored as I have nothing really much to do where as school helps my problem.

This effort to explore the values of two different places is at its most balanced in:

Yes. I think school only sees only the good half of you, and can make a different picture of what you may become, rather than at home where you tend to live more free, and your parents can build a different picture of you.

And perhaps at its most insightful by the child who says

If you don't get on at home you don't get on at school. If you get on at home you get on at school

in contrast with the youngster who is not aware of how much, at both best and worst, the two halves of his life interact:

The pushes you into one thing, the other into another its like being a bloody cable car these days!

Finally, the large number who sense no tension at all between the two environments divide fairly evenly between those who approve, and those who disapprove, of the efforts of both. The disapprovers are resentful of the entire adult world and its values:

My parents aggree with what the school teachers morally. I can't say I do, though.

Both the school and at home half the time they work together. They make you do things you don't want to.

I think they both agree more or less, but what they want I do not.

Or, more cryptically,

I don't care what kind of person they want me to become but I'm going to become it.

How do I know what sort of a person they want me to be? They can't make me something I'm not.

The approving ones report a situation it would not be unfair to describe as the teacher's dream:

My mum and dad say did you enjoy school today and if I say No they start lecturing me about how I should like school and to work hard when I do already.

Not rearly my perants know the teachers know best.

And perhaps the parent's dream, too:

Luckily I have marvellous parents and I feel they are trying to do the same for me as the school is.

One happy youngster holds the whole tension, the pressure on his growth, his growth against the pressure, his elders' hopes and his own sense of final responsibility:

Of course they both want me to become a good person. They both also give me advice but the decision is up to me. Both want you to do the best you can and make the most of this time, they both keep telling me that in the long run you'll thank yourself if you wark hard now.

For him and the large number like him, we must feel that the 'bloody cable car' was an exaggerated image. And we must feel that the notion of a generation in revolt against a combined parent-teacher tyranny is unsubstantiated. Considering how often it is necessary for the sheer survival of our children that we have to stop them doing 'what they want to', it is cheering that only 13% chose this as the most significant thing about school and home life; and that even among these protesters there is often a rueful, reluctant readiness to see that they do not yet know everything, even about the business of being a person.

3 *Punishment*

Do you think punishments have any effect on people?

Yes, they make you *worse*. If the teacher shows you up before the whole class you think, Oh blow 'er, I shall keep on talking. If she asks you nicely after the lesson to be a bit more quiet, you might.   A ☐

Do you think punishments are useful?

> Yes, I think you've got to have them. If you had
> no punishments at all then school would be
> just a wild madhouse.   B ☐

> Well, if you get punished I think it makes you
> more reluctant to work. But if you realise, your
> own self, in your own mind, that you must work,
> to get a good job, and everything, for your parents'
> sake, you do work. Better than being punished.   C ☐

Have you learnt anything because of being punished
for a mistake?

Do you think some children need punishment?

RESULTS

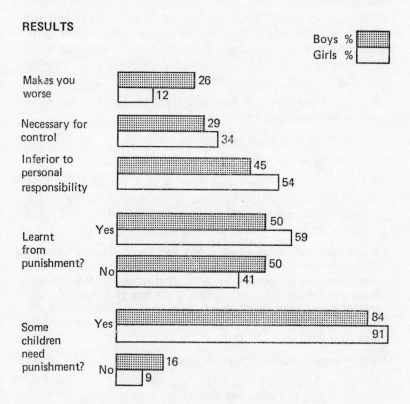

As has happened before, the choices offered were not mutually exclusive. Most teachers, after all, would subscribe to all these statements. 'Yes,' they would say, 'punishment often *does* make rebels more rebellious, at least for the time being. But they are necessary as a final frontier for order. But again yes, what we all want is that our pupils should "realize in their own *minds* that they must work".' All the questions do for our respondents is to ask for a quick grouping according to their first, immediate response to the idea of punishment. Do they hate it and regard it as wholly harmful? Do they see it as the final frontier, to be accepted as necessary? Or are they prepared to argue reasonably about it? A quarter of the boys and a tenth of the girls decide that 'it makes you worse'; but it will be noticed that when they are pushed a little further some of the rebel boys must be among the 84% who decide that *some* children, though presumably not they themselves, need punishment.

The only surprising figure here is the large number, half the boys and two-fifths of the girls, who say they have themselves learnt nothing from being punished. Even the most libertarian adult would admit that punishments can teach *something*; if only caution – as, indeed, one of our respondents observes:

> Yes, you know that next time you might be punished for doing something wrong and you are more wary.

> Yes, to think before I speak.

> Yes, and I'll do that mistake again but I won't be seen this time.

What seems to have happened here is that the children have answered the question in the light of some vivid memory of a particular occasion when the punishment went astray, and when we might want to say it deserved to go astray:

> Yes, I was made to stand on a desk and shout, 'I am a cheat'. I copied one sum in Primary School. I was 8. This was too harsh, I was scared to go to school for weeks afterwards, I kept being sick. Finally my parents realised something was worrying me, and made me tell them. My mother visited the teacher and explained I was scared to go to school, so the teacher spoke to me, and we have been friends since.

One boy speaks from more ample experience:

> No I have been caned twiced been to court 4 time's and I'm only now becoming less noise and villant.

A number make the point that all that is learnt is hostility:

No and it made Me realy hate the teacher.

No I just thought the teacher was picking on me.

No. It makes them hate. Hate the teachers. Hate the school. And everybody else.

I've learnt that I am now scared sick of some teachers.

We cannot press the statistics too hard, here, but the evidence is sadly clear that a good deal of punishment is applied without understanding, and that many of our children have grasped the point at issue. Among those who accept the necessity of a defence against the 'wild madhouse' there are several to point out that mere punishment is of little avail. People must be punished, they agree,

> so they dont think they can do anything they want or have anything they want, but punishment is useless without a talk or something afterwards.

> If someone beening punished for something they done wrong its do them good if you tell them what right what is wrong ... Do not punished someone without any reason because I know some people do.

There is something touching about the strong desire they express for being reasoned with, for having things explained, for being trusted to see for themselves in good time.

> I experimented with a fag and I remember dad saying, 'If I ever catch you with a fag in your mouth I'll tan your arse till your'e black and blue.' I've never stopped smoking. If he had explained the dangers of smoking and *advised* me not to, I might have taken notice.

The reasoning may range from the old-fashioned 'good talking-to' –

> Corporal and physical punishment is wrong. I think it is 10 times more effective if you have a headmistress like ours who just talks sharply to you. I once had a talking-to by her and believe me, I've changed my ways for the better

to a more personal effort to discover what has gone wrong:

> I don't think children need punishment like the cane or the slipper. I think if they are talked to, and asked why they did the thing they did, and you understand, They will try not to do it again, because you have told them that it is wrong, and why they should not do it again.

A few children grasp the point that a psychologist would wish to make, that a continual offender is more in need of treatment than of punishment:

> If they are partically bad and never do What they are told there is something disturbing them.

Those who see the necessity of punishment as the over-riding consideration include those who have learnt from it themselves:

> Yes. I onece forgot to do my homework and I was punished by having a detention for nerly an Hour so I never forgot to do it again.

> Yes, if I didn't get punished I would just be a spoiled brat.

And they include, too, those who perhaps have learnt nothing themselves, but want justice and order to be enforced:

> They Could in there own stupidity jepardice the safety of Someone else. Some really are trouble Makers Example Chris Cross of 3M Hes a real Trouble Maker.

The school needs to punish, say some, because the home has failed:

> Some children need punishing at school because their behaviour reflects in their work which has come from their home. It is their upbringing mostly that makes them so bad at school and if the teacher punishes you, then it is the same as your parents doing it, but they don't.

And such children must be punished, it is argued, when they indulge in really disturbing activity:

> disturbbing someone esles pleasure

> going around smashing kids up

> damaging property for no reason

> children who would hit the teacher or disterb the class so no one else can hear

> those who are cheeky and rude to teachers deserve punishment.

It is not a picture, all this, of children demanding total permissiveness. They ask for order, and for order that asserts itself. But they want it to be just, and compassionate, and personal; and when it is none of these things, they would say, the order is worse than the permissiveness. They are not far, it might be said, from the root of the matter.

4 *Religious education*

What about RE, then? Has that had any influence on you?

No, I'm so bored I don't listen half the time.   A ☐

Loving thy neighbour, it's lovely that you should strive for it, but it's very difficult. It makes it easy to get so discouraged.   B ☐

A lot of people wouldn't get RE at home, so the school would be the place to learn it.   C ☐

I don't think you should have RE. I'm just wanting to learn maths and English and all that to help me in my future.   D ☐

Attitudes to religious education considered as *religious* education have already been sufficiently documented. The object of this enquiry was limited to the possible moral effect of religious education. It would still be argued by many teachers, and assumed without argument by many members of parliament, that the area of learning labelled 'RE' contained somewhere within it, and was possibly – in the present climate of opinion – justified, by some kind of moral growth.

The children were invited to respond to four different, though again not completely distinct, propositions. In order of hostility to religious education, they would go as follows.

D. Religion is irrelevant to the purposes of education, which are concerned with the tools of living.

A. Religion is boring.

B. Religion is splendid, but its ideals are so unattainable that the result is depressing rather than educative.

C. People should know about religion, and if the home no longer teaches it, the school should.

The statements offered did not include specific reference to moral outcomes, but they were included towards the end of a 'moral' questionnaire, and were headed 'The influence of RE'. We cannot assume, therefore, that our respondents thought out their answers in specifically moral terms, but we can, nevertheless, infer that if they find religious education irrelevant and boring in general, they find it irrelevant to moral education.

RESULTS

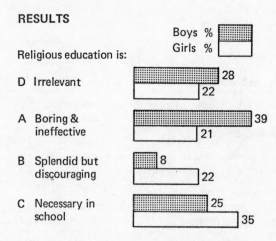

If we further group these already very rough responses into broadly *for* religious instruction (B & C) and broadly *against* (D & A), we have

Boys *for*	33%	Boys *against*	67%
Girls *for*	57%	Girls *against*	43%

On the face of it, these figures lead to no firm conclusion except that we should be unwise to determine the curriculum by democratic vote among fifteen-year-olds. When we look behind the face, to the individual comments, we are offered no firmer guidance, but some food for thought.

The first group are clear and forthright:

Who wants to know about bloody religion.

I thinkes that it all codswallop.

No. I'm an atheist. I suppose I'm stubborn but I don't need religion. I'm happy without it.

A few of them show that they have taken our implicit question about moral influence:

No I don't believe in the Bible and so don't get guidance from it. My parents are pretty good – so I don't need a myth to grow up straight.

My mum does not oppose church, but does not really believe in God. Yet she is the best kindest most loving woman I know and has never and never will break the 10 Commandments.

Religious absolutes are seen as in some way an invasion of the development of authentic personality:

> No I like to form my own standards, not have someone trying to drum theirs into me.

The complaint of boredom often springs from Bible-based teaching that does not speak to the children's condition.

> No because the main topic we took was pesecusion of the Christains.

> The RE we were taught was nothing about moral goodness only about bible stories we've heard over and over again.

One child, himself favourably disposed, thus sees the problem as one of good teaching and a good teacher:

> I enjoyed RE – probably because of a marvellous teacher and an interesting course – however the fact that RE is compulsory – outdated for many modern youngsters and not bothered about at home makes it very different. Unless there is a modern likeable and knowledgeable teacher for such a controversial subject – there are bound to be problems misunderstandings and resentments.

So that some are prepared to say, as was reported so emphatically in *Teenage Religion*, that the discussion-situation will solve the problem:

> Yes, when we have discussions but not otherwise, i.e. not from the bible.

Or there may be hope, some say, in a broad-based religious course designed towards freedom of personal choice:

> I don't think RE should be taught in school and I find the lessons boring. Being taught RE in school has turned me more against being religious. In the lessons I would rather be taught about several different religions and then decide which one seemed right rather than have one that you either have to believe or sit their getting bored.

But one laconic youngster sees no hope in any of it:

> RE at our school is just about stories of what happened in the days of Moses ect. And in the 4th and 5th year you talk about jobs ect

which seems to put *Teenage Religion* in its place.

There are few boys, but a substantial number of girls, to probe the area of conscience, and voice the view that religious ideals are irrelevant, not because they are not 'right', but because they are impossible to achieve.

> I know we are supposed to be like God etc but it is terribly difficult not to do wrong things, we do learn slowly but surely by our own mistakes and this is the best way. I suppose it is good to have such a shining example but personally I would much rather do love, marriage, freindship etc rather than the Bible and the Commandments as those are necessary for a good life and happiness and we should be taught as much as possible about them.

> Sometimes I feel worse than I really should feel after RE as sometimes I am not the person, that the people in the Bible turn out to be.

A small number think there *is* something to be learned from the challenge of perfection:

> I think people do get moral goodness out of RE. They would get a lot of ideas to live a Better life if they were to listen

while one confesses that he has himself:

> Sometimes I stop and think of the bad things I done.

The last group, defending the school's role in religious education, are not without their reasons. They see the value of a model:

> Yes it shows what type of person and morels you should have.

> RE teaches us how we should live. It is about goodness.

It helps to make moral principles clear.

> You learn what right and wrong and in some cases people change after what they hear and its most for the best.

One of them sees the problem of perfectionism, but wants to encounter it:

> Sometimes, you leave the room telling yourself that your going to change to a better person but it is easier said than done.

Or the mere consideration of the challenge promotes thought:

> It does make me think.

One child grasps the point that religious education is not necessarily an invasion of the person, but may provide the food for personal character building.

Not really, my parents taught me it all from since I was so high, I come from a town in Durham, a mining town, there where everyone was on the same level, God became a help, an encouragement. Goodness is what's in you as well as outside. You took to the rules laid down in front of you, sometimes you question them sometimes you just accept them. RE can't give you the answer really and working them out yourself you may be able to but it's just the way you look at it.

There is nothing in all this that we did not know: that we are faced by a generation that is not prepared to sit down and accept religious education without a good deal of question; but is not yet ready to reject it out of hand. A great deal of it, they would want to say, is 'a complete waiste of time'; but they are not, all of them, sure enough of their own powers to do without some instruction in the field: 'You learn what right and wrong'; 'It does make me think'. But they would all agree that in the end 'goodness is what's in you as well as outside': that the outcome of moral education must be moral insight and not mere moral conformity.

Finally, we may ask, is it possible that the boring irrelevance of the lessons has nevertheless not been in vain? Is there a residuum of idealism clustering round the notion of 'a good Christian'?

A previous study[4] suggested that as recently as 1965 the Christian image held by boys and girls of fifteen was considered 'good, generous, sociable, forgiving, strong-willed, confident, courageous, reliable, and sincere'; and the inference seemed to be that the experience of Christian people which these youngsters had had was a reassuring and inspiring one. Is this still true?

They were presented with three choices:

Is a good Christian different from a good man who isn't a Christian?

I think a good person who isn't a Christian is a
better person.   A ☐

A good Christian follows the Ten Commandments
and then looks down on anybody else, looks
down their noses at them.   B ☐

To live happily and get on with people you must
behave in a Christian way.   C ☐

What is attempted here is a grouping by three attitudes:

A. There is no noticeable difference between Christians and non-

Christians, in the matter of goodness, and therefore the non-Christian may claim credit for extra achievement.

B. Christians are worse than non-Christians, because they follow a narrow moral code and despise other people.

C. The Christian ideal is of some effect. (If the statement is analysed, of course, it may be said to mean no more than 'Christian is a conventional, traditional term for a certain moral ideal', and therefore it would be possible to say Yes to both A and C; but the tone of statement C is more favourable to Christian language than that of B.)

The responses were emphatically, though not unanimously, pro-Christian.

RESULTS

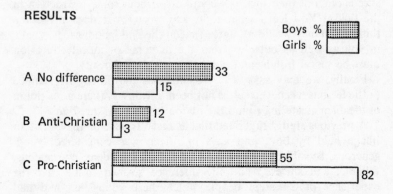

Only 12% of the boys, and 3% of the girls, were aligned against Christians (though it must be borne in mind that despite my defence of these statements as emotional clusterings, they nevertheless *are* statements; and there may be many children who would subscribe to other criticisms of Christians, even though they do not accept this one).

From the tone of their elaborations, though, it is likely that their hostility is fairly wide-ranging:

> I don't know and I don't particularly care! I think that a good Christian is a piddling ponce!

> I think the behaviour of some Christians is absolutely stupid in some cases, all this bible and stuff is a load of ROT.

> Mostley bad.

> Awful.

There is no clue here to the nature of the unhappy experience they generalize from, and we are not to know whether it *is* experience, or merely the repetition of someone else's prejudice. A few, more reasonably, point to the cause of their disapproval:

Well, looking at N. Ireland, not much.

I think that many Christians have forgotten what they are. Many are fighting against each other when there is no need to kill anybody.

A number concurred with the choice offered, and its charge of 'looking down their noses'.

They seem not to understand anyone who isn't a Christian.

I think Christians should treat every one the same, just because they are Christians doesn't mean they know everything.

Stuck up – you can be a good person without believing in God.

At least one seems to be speaking from personal recollection, even though he may have misjudged the situation:

Most of them are hypocrites I feel. OK some people do believe but how many go to Church on Sunday in their best hats, to be seen there? You can always tell the ones, when I used to go to church, some people used to turn round and peer to see who was there. I hate hypocrites especially when it has to do with the Church.

Others are ready to distinguish between one Christian and another, as does this boy, with his dislike of over-pious talk:

It order pends on what kind of Christian this person is, if this person talks about God and religion all the time I think I would get board and walk away. If this person talks about god now an then I would have more time with him ... I don't believe in Christians, I think they are too religious.

Indeed the use of religious language, with its implication of an in-group claiming special revelations, causes a good deal of anger:

If someone doesn't agree with what they say about God the Christian starts getting very viscous like one girl in our class.

And others, not so hostile, level the charge that Christians so often fail to live up to their own ideals:

Its no good calling yourself a Christian *then* trying to live up to it. You've got to prove your good enough before you can safely say that you are a Christian.

Not everybody are good Christians. Even good Christians do things wrong.

This point is made with more sympathy by some who have responded to the third statement.

Christananity is misused in many ways but theres nothing wrong with Christians.

Real christians I think are those who are always ready to help other people but really they are no different except their very easy to get on with.

By their fruits, some of them would say if they remembered their 'bible and stuff'; active Christian concern is to be commended, pious idling is not:

As long as they act in human ways and not on a stool all day there alright.

A few, a very few, seem to speak from experience of actual Christians who have impressed them in some way.

A Christian has this sense of happiness. They are willing and even in hard times they manage to fight through. They have got a warm feeling of encouragement and satisfaction.

The group who decide there is no difference between Christians and non-Christians, though not the most numerous, is the most fluent, seeing the problem, and spreading themselves most amply in teasing it out. They see the problem – which many Christians would see as the first problem – of deciding what a Christian is.

I Don't really know what the behaviour of a true Christian is, whether it's believing in God and going to church every week or whether it's someone who is always good and kind to everyone and never says a wrong word to anyone or about anyone.

In this situation, many wish to attach the word 'Christian' to a person with a certain set of beliefs, and use 'good man' for general moral insight and conduct; and conclude that the question of belief is irrelevant.

You don't have to be a Christian to be a kind and loving person. I think that a Christian is no different to any other person. It is just that they believe in something which others don't.

Stupid: Yo do not have to be a Christian to be a good person.

Christians behave like everyone else except they believe in a faith

which they are influenced by. To be a good Christian you must obey
the 10 Commandments and the laws of the church. But even if a
person did not go to Mass or Confession he could still be a good
person. To be a good Christian you must treat others kindly, live a
good life and not harm or hurt anyone.

This last contains an important piece of analysis. The Christian
ethic can have two totally different meanings: ritual and moral laws
specifically laid upon Christians by reason of their accepting the
authority of the church, including such things as church-going, the
duty of prayer, and the current ecclesiastical decisions on such
matters as abortion; or it may mean a general ethic applicable to
all men, whether or not they accept the metaphysic of the Christian
faith. The controversy over these last would turn on the question
of whether such general laws are derived from Christian insight or
whether they are in some existential way built in to the human
situation, discoverable by any honest man. One girl, obviously
writing from inside the Christian tradition and valuing it, sees the
point:

> In some cases christians do good, they help the poor and needy,
> eg as misionarys, but sometimes their believe becomes an absesion,
> then they think *everybody* should believe in God and those who
> don't are bad people, even uneducated. Good people are Christians,
> even if they don't completely believe in God or understand him.
> Everyone at a certain times need God, to blame for the impossible
> or the unexplained. I believe Christ was a good man, I don't believe
> completely in God, all I say is that Christ showed us what to do,
> how to do it, and why to do it, he was a very good man who tried
> to teach others to be too. If we follow as best we can his ways, we
> may be a good person, or christian, whichever way you wish to take
> it.

There is here a reluctance to lose the inspiration of the Christian
ideal, but an equal reluctance to deny the power of the ordinary
human being to live a worthy life. It is a Christian expression of
the humanist spirit, matched by some who warn us of the danger
of being too religious:

> Some people are too Christian. Instead of helping as they are taught
> to, they say this is wrong and that is wrong and become creeps
> and moaners.

> Christians act the same as anyone else, unless they have religious
> mainer.

Or, perhaps more temperately put:

I think the Christian ideals are good but one cannot hope to keep to all of them and lead a normal life.

There lies beneath all this the linguistic muddle, in which adults would be as deeply involved, as to the meaning to be attached to 'Christian'; but there lies also a rather touching hope and longing for goodness, and goodness in very recognizable terms: generosity, imagination, tenderness, spontaneity, and active concern.

Can we help them to make their hope come true?

7

Critique of Moral Education

It is not customary to pay much attention to the views of school pupils on the educational process. Education, we should say, is a deliberate activity by means of which the older, or more learned, or more skilful members of society set out to effect a change in its novices. Only those who are already educated can decide what it means to educate, and therefore to shape the process itself. Of course, we should say, we will take the child himself into account: we will assess his skills, ask him, from time to time, about his preferences, arrange his curriculum in the light of what job he wants to do; we will talk, sincerely and seriously, about child-centredness and self-realization, about developing his interests and giving him freedom for discovery. But when we have gathered all our information about him, it remains at best data for our decision-making. We seize on his declared interests and exploit them for other ends; we watch his use of his freedom, call him back when he goes too far in what we consider a dead-end or a dangerous path; and even when we decide to let him run some risks, it is we who decide what those risks shall be. He knows, as well as we do, that his life is a playing at reality: that his decisions are mock decisions, because we shall prevent him from making a totally wrong choice. We do not ask an English baby whether he would prefer English or Spanish as his first language; we do not let him discover what it is like to fall off a cliff.

The uneducated, we say, cannot decide what education is, and it follows therefore that the half-educated cannot be taken very seriously when they pass judgment about what is happening to them. Education is to be finally judged by its outcomes, and what can be the worth of views expressed before there can be any outcomes? We do not wake up a patient in the middle of an operation to ask if he feels better: why should we listen to fifteen-year-olds on the middle stages of our educational surgery?

As a final statement on the matter, a sort of ultimate educational commandment, this is no doubt impregnable. But final statements are never quite the whole statement. We may recite the commandment but, to borrow the words of one of our boys on commandments, there must be 'a lot more sidetracks to it'. Even in the teaching of a formal skill, where the teacher really knows and the pupil is really ignorant, the purposes of the pupil, the way he sees the skill as something he can use, are a basic element in the learning process. 'You taught me your language,' says Caliban, 'and the profit on't Is I know how to curse.' What he wants it for *now*, not at some unseen future, is an active reality at every stage. So this educational playing must be playing at *reality*, and not playing at playing; and within the real bounds on freedom there must be real freedom. A true seeking for the pupil's response then becomes part of true teaching, which becomes a response to a response. In the words of an Oxford report on student discipline:

> Listen to your students. I mean really listen. If we do not listen they are going to find some other way to attract our attention ... A university in which the existence and exercise of authority create among its students a sense that the university is divided into 'Them' and 'Us' is a howling wilderness where no academic purposes can prosper.[5]

What is true of academic purposes is even more urgently relevant to moral purposes, for moral skills exist – begin and flourish – in a relationship of personal identities. The identity of the learner is present in his first learning of his basic trust: a shapeless identity at first of bowels and limbs and fleshly comfort and random shouts, but a genuine identity of loving and being loved. The moral educator, making his necessary plans from the position of authority that he cannot abdicate, thus has to listen for his pupils' response. He cannot even make his plans without some listening and, more urgently, he cannot carry them out. The task itself is relating and establishing relations; and the relation of identities is not to be achieved by smothering one of the identities involved.

This point our young people have grasped. Their only doubt about it is whether *we* have. The girl who replied to the question about 'the art of living' with 'We've only had two lessons' was firmly taken to task: lessons in the art of living, the others told her, aren't necessary to learning about living.

> You're *born* to get on with people. They can't change something inside of you to make you get on with people. You can be a friendly

sort of person, but school lessons can't change you like that.

We should want to qualify this. Birth is important, but it is not the end of the story; and older folk are not as powerless as they think to 'change something inside', if they are so disposed. But in essence, these children are right. They warn us off the holy ground of the person, as he reasons and reflects, and is conscious of continuing identity. Even my fairly gentle questioning drew 'none of you Bisness', and there is a widespread fear of pressures towards somebody else's model of personality.

They defend, then, their identity; but they see themselves, nonetheless, as growing and developing. It is the same 'I' who watches and suffers and remembers, and sustains existence; but it is a growing 'I', with some of the growth a secret matter beyond anyone's control. 'You grow up anyhow, eventually ... We've matured a bit. We don't prance around giggling, do we? When you see the first years now you sort of think, aren't they childish?' What they are saying here is, 'We are not puppets, to be put through our moral paces by other fingers. You may think you manipulate us, but at bottom, it is not so.'

> How do *I* know what sort of person they want me to be. They can't make me something I'm not.

And so they admit to change, but not, at a radical level, a change determined by others. 'It's not school, really.'

Teachers may shy at this, fearing their role to be threatened. If 'it's not school really', then why bother with schools at all? But they are not, these young folk, raising that sort of question: they are simply asserting that when the story is told of all that goes on around them, calling forth, much of it, a personal response, the person who responds remains ultimately himself.

At this point, if we were so minded, we could be flooded by questions. There are philosophical difficulties in the appalling vagueness of every word I use. There are psychological and biological difficulties about stimulus and response, and growth and development. There are sociological difficulties about culture and identity. If we try to attach a precise meaning to talk about 'a person remaining ultimately himself' we shall soon be compelled to retire defeated. But these young people are not attempting a descriptive statement of a psychological and sociological state of affairs, so much as putting up a warning notice saying 'Keep Off!' And when they say 'They can't make me something I'm not' they are saying

'I'm not going to let them . . .' We should be wise to take the warning seriously, whatever be the facts of the case.

But this is not to say that there is nothing for the old to do at all, or that personal identity can grow and flourish without any help, or that it must be sheltered from any kind of alien influence. Identity is discovered and developed, but it is not simply made up. Persons do not spin the web of their being from their own entrails: they learn to spin by being taught to spin, and the matter for their spinning is given, much of it deliberately, by other persons.

At this point we run into a question that has recently caused a good deal more trouble, I believe, than it deserves.

I am thinking of a widespread and extreme tenderness towards individuality, as good in itself, appearing in many guises and many contexts. It appears in much of the advocacy of discovery-methods, where it seems more important that children should discover something, even if it is wrong, than that they should be led towards something that happens to be right. It appears in talk about growth and development, and self-expression and child-centredness. It turns up in arguments on the neutrality of the teacher. And it turns up, with the widest spine-chilling effect, when anybody uses the word 'indoctrination'.

'Indoctrination' is now a straightforward boo-word, used to pick out a practice of plain evil – this despite its honourable ancestry as a word that meant simply to teach well: 'to imbue with learning', as the OED nobly puts it. Nowadays it means, equally simply, 'to teach wickedly', 'to-teach-with-something-wrong-about-it'. There seems to be no longer any doubt, in the general usage, that this is what the word conveys. The only doubt is what it refers to, precisely which 'something-wrong' is being identified. The extreme form of it is easy enough to recognize: it is to persuade somebody that a falsehood is true. And there is no difficulty about recognizing this. A dictator, telling the people a lie three times over because it then becomes truth; a teacher persuading his pupils that a particular religious sect has a monopoly of truth, a parent persuading his children that the police are bogey-men (or students persuading each other that they are pigs): these are all indoctrinating. If they make use of painful persuasion (such arguments as match-sticks up the finger-nails) or hypnotism or drugs, we should say they are brain-washing. The difference between indoctrination and brainwashing seems to be only a matter of method and degree. They both represent points on a scale of 'teaching-boo-ness'.

Then the question arises, What is the difference between teaching-hurrah and teaching-boo? How can we distinguish between teaching and indoctrination? For if teaching falsehood as truth is the mark of indoctrination, we get into difficulties over the teaching of controversial matters, or unproved matters, as truth. If the test is truth/falsehood, then we are entitled to apply the word indoctrination to the teaching of any sort of proposition with which we disagree. It thus becomes indoctrination to bring up Russian children to be good Russians, but it is education to bring up English children to be good Englishmen, unless you happen to be Welsh or Scottish, in which case it may become indoctrination again. If we stick to the truth-falsehood test, indeed, the verb is to be conjugated: 'I teach; thou indoctrinatest; he brainwashes.'

Some teachers have developed such a tender conscience about the possibility of indoctrinating in this way that they have almost been rendered incapable of teaching at all. A history teacher tells us how he gave up teaching in school because he 'did not want to teach about May Day in Shakespeare's England ... or the causes of the Hundred Years' War' and so began to teach Liberal Studies to technical college students, turning his attention to more manly themes such as the rise of the Labour Party and the origin of the welfare state. But here, he says

> I felt that I was treading on dangerous ground. How far was I getting my students consciously or unconsciously to share my own political beliefs, however carefully I stuck to the 'facts'? And if they did come to share them was I not indoctrinating them, not educating them? In my very selection of topics to include these political issues was I not doing with different content what a planner of a history syllabus in Soviet Russia does – and wasn't this indoctrination? [6]

Driven to the decision that he could no longer honestly teach about the welfare state, this teacher went off to an institute of education to teach philosophy. But if it is indeed the case, that history cannot be taught without indoctrinating, and if indoctrinating is wicked, then the teaching of history is wicked. This seems a curious conclusion to have reached; and it is clear that we must get out of it.

Let us return to the consideration of what we might mean when we use the word indoctrination. We mean some kind of persuasion used by a teacher to make his pupils accept an idea that they have not arrived at by rational reflection on their own experience. The difference between indoctrination and good teaching would then be said to lie in the presence – in good teaching – of reflection on experience. Now as a statement of the *opposition* between teaching and indoctrination, this is reasonably satisfactory. We can see what is being meant, and can without much difficulty agree with it. But it is not so helpful when we try to draw a line down the middle, and say that all teaching based on rational procedures is good teaching, while all teaching that omits some part of the rational argument required is bad teaching, or indoctrination – this is not so clear.

I am not now thinking of the necessity we certainly labour under of giving children warnings without the full reasons for them: don't touch the switch, don't pull pussy's tail, and so on – because we are not indoctrinating here; we are simply commanding. Nor am I thinking of the problem that when a child asks what the moon is made of, we cannot give him all the reasons for believing what we do, because we can defend as 'teaching-hurrah' any process that prepares the way for later understanding. Presumably we could also evade this particular difficulty, if we were pedantic about indoctrination, by refusing to answer such questions until the child was old enough to understand; though if we did, he would have a rather boring childhood, and a busy old age catching up.

A much more fundamental difficulty, however, awaits us. If I decide, reasonably enough, that sports are good for the health, and command my child to take part in them; then so far, it may be said, I am not indoctrinating. I am deciding reasonably, and commanding. But as soon as I decide which sport he shall engage in first, I import a value-system into his life, in which the relative values of different sports will be permanently affected. I cannot say, 'I want you to be open-minded about sports until you are old enough to choose for yourself,' because until he has reached a certain level of skill and has actually enjoyed a sport, he cannot have a mind on the subject at all. Until he has enjoyed a satisfactory ski-run he is not a rational judge of whether or not skiing is good for him. But my training of him in skiing has to some degree closed his mind, for I have used up the time he needed to become a successful swimmer or footballer or cricketer; and in the very process of my teaching I have had to employ persuasion towards skiing which acts as a persuasion against swimming and football and cricket. I shall be saying 'lovely, lovely' when my pupil falls over and breaks his arm; I shall be rewarding him with hot drinks when he comes in with frost-bite. And even if I am careful about such persuasion, and do not lie too exorbitantly, by the very choice of skiing as the first sport to learn I have made, and conveyed to him, a value-judgment of some sort which must affect him all his life. My enthusiasm may be counter-productive, and make him loathe skiing for the rest of his life : but it has done something to him. And I could not really justify all my efforts by saying that I wanted him to learn to *choose*: it only makes sense if I say, and mean what I say, that I want him to learn to ski.

There seems to be no escape from this dilemma, that either to teach or not to teach is to 'indoctrinate'. Teaching anything at all carries the doctrine that this thing matters; not teaching it carries the doctrine that it does not matter; and the first move in the game, of teaching or not teaching, is taken by the teacher, on behalf of his pupil, without any possibility of rational consent by the pupil.

The truth of the matter is that the attempt to identify a practice called 'indoctrination' has been mistaken. The word is a bogey-word used to frighten teachers away from their proper responsibility. There can be good teaching and bad teaching, of course; but indoctrination is not simply teaching-with-something-wrong-about-it. I should, indeed, want to link the words together in the opposite way, and say that teaching-without-indoctrination is bad teaching – provided I am also allowed to distinguish between good indoctrination and bad.

The fundamental reason for this stance arises from the inescapable fact that moral learning goes on in relationship, and cannot go on in any very real sense in any other way. Values are not 'there' in the object or person or choice being considered, susceptible of being graded by a colour-chart. They are a function of at least two persons-in-relation. Valuing, as distinct from liking or plumping, is itself a matter of looking at something with the reality of another person in mind : it is an attempt to respond to an experience or a dilemma *binocularly*. And in the same way the process of learning to value is an inter-personal process, and the learner cannot proceed without in some way being exposed to the indoctrination of another-person-valuing.

I hope I do not need to say, what seems to be obvious, that when I thus endeavour to put the word 'indoctrination' out of circulation, because it is a bogey-word, I do not therefore imply that it would be perfectly in order for a teacher to teach any kind of falsehood, or for him to teach a controversial point of view as if it were the established truth, or to teach truths, however generally agreed, without ever giving reasons, or to teach with the intention of closing pupils' minds instead of opening them. All I am doing, indeed, is making the case that 'indoctrination' is a word like 'killing' and not like 'murder'. 'Murder' means 'killing-with-something-wrong-about-it', while 'killing', though usually thought to be wrong, may sometimes be right. 'Indoctrination' is in the same case as killing: except that I would say not merely that it is sometimes right, but that it is always inevitable; and a non-indoctrinating teacher is not teaching at all. A purely value-free education would be non-communicating, impersonal: it would be education-by-leaving-alone.

But our young folk do not want to be left alone. When somebody used the word 'conscience', and was asked where conscience came from, they said, 'Somebody sets you standards.' 'Who?' 'Your parents.' They made no fuss about this. They accepted the inevitability of the internalization of values instilled from others: they realized they had to be *informed*.

At this radical level, they were not conscious of any profound difference between home and school: both, they argue, support each other, and both influences were necessary for their growth. What they *are* complaining about is simply the failure of both to recognize that by now their own identity is a reality, and that growth must now arise in conversation, in which their own searching and questioning are taken seriously: 'There's no complaint, but I wish ...,' with the wishing being directed to being listened to.

School When they comment on the difference between home and school, they show no fear of radical indoctrination, and merely fasten on either the non-essentials or the inevitable. Uniform and smoking emerge as the first source of irritation. School insists on regulation clothing, school bans smoking; at home you can wear what you like, and some homes (though it would here be an over-simplification to speak of working-class homes) allow smoking. On such issues we should want to say that the differences do not go very deep, unless the actual handling of them drives them deep. In the society in which they are to live, there is a broad understanding that different situations call for different clothes, and there is no harm in the notion that school can call for different clothes from home. The problems that become bitter here arise from the school not listening sufficiently tenderly to children's feelings about detail. Sometimes storms blow up over centimetres of hair-length, or dress-length, but for every headmaster who achieves national fame by sending a pupil home there are a thousand who say, 'I have something more important to do than measure boys' hair.' Similarly, in our society, there is wide agreement that there are some situations in which it is inappropriate to smoke, and there is no harm in declaring the school one of those situations. Here again, trouble arises when an offence against this rule of appropriateness is interpreted as a challenge to authority or as a sign of incorrigible vice. And here again, for one headmaster who makes a serious issue of smoking, there are a thousand who will listen and converse, explaining the point of the rule with sense and without anxiety, and will deal with infringements as he deals with all infringements.

A more radical difference – and here it may be realistic to talk, very generally, of a difference between a middle-class and a working-class background – lies in the pressure to work. When they were asked what the school seemed to think a good person was like, the commonest first response was 'a hard worker'. Some children see no problem here. Their parents want them to work hard too:

> My mum and dad say did you enjoy school today and if I say No they start lecturing me about how I should like school and to work hard

and

> My perants know the teachers know best

and

> I have marvellous parents and I feel they are trying to do the same for me as the school is.

But the gospel of work, as it comes through to these boys and girls, is not always so easy to accept. What the school wants, they say, is to push us along, harder and harder, so that we can do well in exams, have a top place in some firm and earn a lot of money, and take a good position in society

> and if you don't want to make a place in society, well hard luck, but you've still got to.

This degree of wriggling on the hook we might reasonably accept as inevitable, feeling that in between the impossible doctrine that all work is fun and the lamentable doctrine that work is never fun there is a position that work can be less than fun, but can be seen to be worthwhile. They are now learning, we should say, to cope with the sheer *hardness* of work, and will one day, faced by a mortgage or the need to buy a pram, be grateful for the lesson. Some of them already say this:

> It's something you need, really, because you're going to be dependent on yourself.

And they accept the process as tiresome in itself but acceptable:

> for a certain time – till your mind's grown. Teachers sort of run you round and get you to get on with your own work.

The school where that was said had established a particularly good relationship with its pupils, and emerged from the questionnaire with more favourable responses than any other; and on this issue of work it seems to have solved the problem of exerting pressure without threatening personal identity.

> It *is* left to you what you do as far as work is concerned, and if you don't get it in then they sort of hint that you should have got it in. I think it helps you to learn to decide for yourself.

Such tension as exists in a school where that can be said must be accepted as not merely inevitable, but healthy and creative. A working adult accepts the notion that the office or factory is a place for work and home is a place for being himself; and the issue becomes merely one of appropriateness.

In another school, however, a more disconcerting point is made. Poverty begins at school, they say,

> because once you get to the fourth year, if you take academic subjects then teachers push you into better jobs, but if you don't then they sort of leave you alone more, and gradually the pressure gets less and less for you to work hard.

It would be easy for us to object here that they cannot have it both ways, to argue that 'it's better to be poor and happy than rich and sad', and to throw hippies into the discussion, and at the same time complain that if 'you're somebody brainy they push you but if not they don't particularly bother about you'. The teacher might counter by saying that he is pushing those who have the ability to be pushed, and is settling for a situation in which the others can choose to be poor and happy. Inevitably, those who can learn most will require most attention, simply because learning requires attention. Those who want to be hippies, however tentative their decision, are asking not to be bothered with, and cannot seriously complain if they are left to themselves.

But it is doubtful if we could maintain this position. The difference between schools and other institutions of learning, such as universities, lies in the assumption that children cannot, and must not be allowed to, decide in any irrevocable fashion about the shape of their future lives. We cannot stop them making many decisions that will in practice prove irrevocable – unless we smother them, which is irrevocable in a different way. But we can, and do, maintain that until they leave school nobody, neither they nor we, will close any door that can reasonably be kept open. This is part of the case for comprehensive secondary education, and against streaming; it is part of the case for a wide front in the school curriculum; it is part of the case for a restrictive, grandmotherly code of moral regulation. Chastity, prohibition of drugs and smoking, the banning of weapons and the like are sometimes viewed as an invasion of children's rights, but they are meant as defences of the future adult's rights against the self-destructiveness of ignorance and impulse.

Something has gone wrong, therefore, if boys and girls of fifteen gain the impression that they are no longer being bothered with. It is certainly not intentional: the streaming and setting are designed to create situations in which each child will feel himself at home, and be able to work at a pace within his powers. And the 'bottom set' are certainly, whatever its occupants think, 'bothered with'. But the point they make does raise some questions for moral education, questions about school organization and the structure of incentives; questions about curricula and examinations, about teaching methods and teachers' attitudes. In the end, all these questions push into questions about adult society itself, the 'rat-race' with its top and bottom places. These last it is not the business of the school to resolve – and happily so, for the teacher has enough to do without running the world. But unless he asks them, and unless the school's incentive-system chimes with the personal motives of its members, something will go astray.

A still more radical point is made about the difference between home and school, again one that is inevitable and proper, but one that calls for thought. Several children make remarks that imply that there *is* a tension, and that they resolve it in favour of the home. Home is the personal base, school a place in which tools are acquired. Failure at school is therefore less important than failure at home, and while a home failure spells failure all round, school is of secondary importance.

> If you don't get on at home you don't get on at school. If you get on at home you get on at school.

The second part of that statement is demonstrably not always true, but the first part is hardly open to question.

Home is the personal base, and however urgent the adolescent need for escape it remains an indestructible base, from which sallies are conducted, whose strengths and weakness the young person takes into battle with him. Home, as T. S. Eliot put it, is where you start out from. And our boys and girls know it.

They know, too, something about the effect on school performance of social-class differences. They use their own language here: distinguishing not by socio-economic categories but by O and A levels, making the point that those parents who have passed successfully through the system themselves will have a different attitude to school values from those who failed, or never wanted to succeed. They make here the point with which sociologists have made us familiar, that 'educated' parents are more likely to support the school than 'uneducated'. But they make a further distinction. The O and A level parents are not *certain* to support the school, because

if parents are more intelligent, they can see more flaws in their arguments.

Educational argument is so often conducted on the assumption that where there is any conflict between school and home it is the school that will be right, and the parents wrong, that it is healthy to be reminded that there are occasions when it is the school that is wrong. Parents who are teachers themselves need no reminding of this, when their own children run into avoidable trouble, and they suspect that somewhere a teacher is failing to treat their child as a person.

Teachers teach you, but they don't care so much ... My father cares a lot more about what I become. But at school they don't really care. There are a few who do. But the majority don't.

The truth is that there are no safe generalizations to be made. The child who said that teachers were not involved also said, 'not that I blame them', and to be realistic about this, we should have to admit that the whole situation would be impossible if teachers *were* involved in the way parents are. It is a fearsome thought, to contemplate what school life would be like if they were.

Furthermore, it would not be an educative situation. The adolescent task is to discover personal identity as a tool-user and a role-performer, choosing the skills and the tasks which develop and express true potential, and maintaining within them a tolerable degree of consistency. It is the substitution of an integrity derived from the security of parental values by the inner security of personal values, created and sustained from within against a range of pressures from without. To this end, the cooler relationships of school are an essential means to the making of decision. 'Teachers are strangers really ... You try things on with them.' And without *some* degree of trying things on with relative strangers, there can be no hope of stability in a life that must be lived among 'strangers really'.

The ground on which all relationships, both at home and school, exist is a ground of basic trust: the home creates it and makes it possible, the school sustains it. But if we were to try to discriminate between the tasks of home and school we should point to the personal relationship, face to face and total, as the over-riding gift of the home, and that of the schools a safe structure of relationships, cooler, continuous, and just. Our young people do not want the school to count for too much; but equally they do not want it to cease to count at all. They are really making this point when they point the difference between the primary school and the secondary school, arguing that

> Primary schools don't give children enough responsibility in an individual trust in each other, and they're told what to do, they're expected to do it; and then they get to secondary school and they're suddenly expected to behave well ... There's too big a gap between them.

We would have more to say about this, but they are right in the claim that there is a curious shock in moving from a close-knit family-group based on a classroom home to an almost nomadic existence in which tribes of children move every hour from one ruler to another, and have to evolve an eclectic ethos that will cope with the differences between tyrants.

They are not complaining, however, that the secondary school fails in its overall task. They appreciate that it is a place for a certain kind of work, and they accept it.

> Teachers sort of run you round and get you to get on with your own work ... They put pressure in a good way ... I've no objections to working hard.

And even when the work seems pointless to their individual purposes, and they 'did work they knew they were going to give up afterwards', they saw that the school had a responsibility to introduce them to the ways of human thought: 'it's to tell you what you want to know'.

The role of the secondary school, they would say, is the provision of a situation in which persons meet each other, and discover their own identity in relation. They vote against the notion that the school doesn't help in growth at all, but merely 'stops you going downward'. They vote more strongly for the notion that its main task is 'to help you to mix'; and the majority see the gift of school life as the attainment of 'our own view-points' from the time when they 'took what teacher said for granted ... Now we argue it.'

The question to be asked here is how much serious weight is placed on the word 'argue'. If 'argue' means merely contradict, or air one's own opinions, there is not much more to be said for it than for 'not arguing' or learning to conform to received opinion. Neither of these is entirely valueless: received opinions are often worth receiving; and the opportunity of airing one's own is an opportunity of engaging in a secure relationship, and of actually listening to one's own opinions in a public situation. But if we want attitude-change of any kind, it seems that exhortation does very little, and the haphazard expression of unexamined thoughts does none at all. What actually works is to engage people in a situation where they are not afraid to say what they think, but equally not afraid to subject it to examination, and to bring their thinking to the scrutiny of other minds in the light of some public criteria of argument. Good teaching, even of highly structured material such as is handled in elementary science, turns not on statements to be accepted, but on questions to be answered: Do you see? Do you really see it for yourself? And in the cloudier territory of morality, there is no gain to be hoped for from statements, but much from searching questioning.

It is a questioning of both teachers and fellow-pupils. Of teachers, one of our boys said.

> Some are OK to talk to, but there are the stiff ones who believe kids have no minds of their own.

And so, said another,

> We turned to each other – we were all in the same boat so we had nothing to be shy of.

This could stand, could it not, as the crucial statement of the role of the school as a place of talk: that it should be a place in which teachers are OK to talk to, and in which the discussion of serious issues is conducted in an open friendliness and freedom from restraint that permits boys and girls to turn to each other. It is true, in a poignant way that older folk often forget, that the young *are* in the same boat. Their elders have, admittedly, been through a good deal of what they are going through; but they have not been through precisely the same thing. They went through it with another set of parents and teachers, and in another world; and they view their experience with hindsight. They are entitled to be listened to, but in the end they cannot know exactly what it means to be young in the present world, and to be entering a new one without foresight. For at bottom, there is no foresight. 'Children dwell in the house of tomorrow, into which we cannot enter.' It is their identity they have to discover, and carry forward into responsibility; and they can only discover it in the give-and-take of a mutual relationship. 'You have,' said one of them, as he appraised the value of his school life,

> you have mixed with many people so you have got used to how to get on with the different types of people. We have built up to stick up for what we belife.

There is, however, another side to all this. It is true that the objective of the school is the development of identity; and that this is something that children must make for themselves. But it is also true that the school is a *preventive* agency, charged with the duty of making certain kinds of discovery impossible. When the state first began legislating against child-labour, it found that enforcement was made easier by compelling children to go to school; and there is still a protective function for the schools to perform. 'You will not', we say to our children, 'explore what it is like to steal and assault, to fornicate or get drunk; and we shall not let you uproot the foundations of school order. Some things we want you to seek for, because only your seeking can win you the finding. In your seeking, you will make mistakes, and we shall forgive them. But there are some things you must not seek for at all; and if you do we shall punish you. You are, in the end, under the discipline of our authority.'

The merely negative and protective role of discipline and punishment, as a 'wall of brass' round our children's lives, needs no defence, and is not difficult, in practice, to maintain. But can we say it is morally educative, in any positive sense? And, in particular, can punishment be said to reform?

School discipline It is not unknown for the discussion of discipline and punishment to go on as if they are virtually the same thing. One of the senses offered by the dictionary, indeed, is 'correction; chastisement; the mortification of the flesh by penance; also a beating, or the like'. Between this narrow sense and the un-handy and over-general sense of 'instruction imparted to disciples or scholars; teaching; learning; education', there lies an area of reference of more direct application: 'the training of scholars and subordinates to proper conduct and action by instructing and exer-cising them in the same ... the order maintained and observed among persons under control or command; a system of rules for conduct'. It is probably this area to which teachers would normally refer when they talk about discipline; and it is an area of obvious concern to moral education.

'Training, order maintained, and rules for conduct' covers that aspect of school life in which children are told how to behave and habituated to it, how they are prevented from misbehaviour and corrected when it occurs, and how rules are laid down, made clear, and enforced in such a way that children can be free from the indi-vidual tyranny of either stronger children or brutal staff, and can learn to make decisions in the light of probable consequences.

Now it is plain that there can be a perfectly adequate system of discipline without the concept of punishment appearing at all. A school which had a system of rules, and explained them, and cor-rected breaches of the rules by conversation with offenders, could well be described as having an adequate system of discipline. In practice, most schools do contain an element of punishment, and would defend it as necessary in the realities of the teaching situa-tion, and – though perhaps with less conviction – as educative and reformatory. Our boys and girls were asked to talk only about punishment, and not about discipline in the wider sense, because it is at the moment of punishment that the system of order really bites. There is among them so little disposition to doubt the necessity of a certain minimum of order that questions about this are not worth asking; but inevitably they question the necessity of a deliberate process of the infliction of pain.

Approximately a fifth doubt whether it has any value at all. It makes you worse, they say:

> It makes them hate. Hate the teachers. Hate the school. And every-body else.

This group believe that nobody needs punishment. They may admit that some people are finally untameable, but these should be 'thrown out of the school'. Four-fifths, however, are willing to concede the case for punishment as a necessity for the survival of a community. A third, indeed, pick on this as the most important thing to be said:

> Yes, I think you've got to have them. If you had no punishments at all then school would just be a wild madhouse.

They support their case on grounds of sheer expediency, because the memory of punishment serves as a deterrent ('next time you are more wary') or, more cynically, as a deterrent against being caught. And they have in mind, as offences calling for punishment, violence against property or persons ('going around smashing kids up') or the kind of behaviour that prevents the school from fulfilling its purposes ('children who would hit the teacher or disterb the class so no one else can hear'). 'Some really are trouble Makers' they say, who 'Could in there own stupidity jepardice the safety of Someone else'.

This widespread, if faintly reluctant, support for the system does not, of course, settle the issue. All they are saying here is that order must be preserved, and if that demands painful correction, then painful correction there must be. They are not here arguing, as adults often do after an unusually sordid murder, that the offender 'deserves what's coming to him'. And there is, after all, considerable support for the notion that punishment, by making the offender angry, in practice fails in its object. A happy and co-operative community is not created by increasing hate among its members. Further, they say, certain kinds of misbehaviour spring from causes to which the notion of punishment is inapplicable:

> If they are partically bad and never do What they are told there is something disturbing them.

And here, they would go on to argue, even the maintenance of order demands not punishment but treatment.

They do not settle the issue, then, of punishment and the decision to use it; but they do settle the question we might ask as to whether punishment of a sort is broadly acceptable. If the teenage generation were as hostile to all authority as we are sometimes told, it might be the case that the mere presence of punishment in a school would so corrupt the atmosphere that it could be defended only on negative grounds, as a mere survival-mechanism. But our young people do not take this view. They are, in their present mood, ready to accept its presence without protest.

What they do ask is that we should consider its purposes, and punish only for those purposes.

Do not punished someone without any reason *because I know some* people do.

Now the obvious purpose is the one already discussed, the erection of a system of deterrents against the kind of conduct that disrupts community. But this purpose may well come into conflict with the particular purposes of the *school* community, which are concerned with education. After all, the simplest way of eliminating destructive behaviour in schools would be to abolish schools; and it would be easy to control 'children who would hit the teacher' by sitting at a desk with a gun. And in the context of moral *education* we must always be asking questions about the long-term, as well as the short-term, effects on personality of our devices for control. When a teacher punishes, he does more than punish: he teaches. Leaving aside the possibility of punishing one offender without any hope of changing him, but merely in order to 'teach' the rest of the class (which could obviously be defensible in certain circumstances) the nagging question for the teacher is 'What is this punishment expected to teach the victim?' One of our young folk started up the thought that it would teach 'respect' for the teacher; but he was soon talked down:

It's teaching people to bow down, isn't it? .. If you hit them hard enough they're going to be respectful to you, aren't they?

All *I* learnt, said another, was to be 'scared sick of some teachers'.

The notion of learning 'respect', however, may have more in it than they were immediately prepared to see. 'If you respect your teacher, you won't try to do the things you would get punished for'. Respect here carries the meaning of 'deferential esteem'; and while none of us would question the proposition that esteem for a person in authority is of value in establishing a relationship, it could also be said that the note of deference is also of value. An act of punishment, considered by itself, would seem only to teach respect for the teacher's power; and the question arises as to why we should bother to teach this at all. 'It doesn't help you in the long run'. But in the short run, if this is not acknowledged, it *has* to be learnt. The teaching situation, as we have seen, is not an equal relationship but a relationship of authority and dependence, and if it is not seen as such by the pupil, he cannot be established as a learner. 'Who are you, you powerless one,' he might say, 'to tell me I am wrong?'

Of course, we should want to say, the teacher must not *simply* assert his power. His punishment must be in support of more positive purposes than this. But then the power itself is only legitimate in support of those purposes. If it is exercised for a genuine purpose, there is something to be learnt about the reality of the power. Most of us find ourselves uneasy, using language like this, which seems to support the notion of an overt display of power; but few of us, perhaps, would be easy with the notion that power should never be displayed at all. The teacher who cannot enforce the purposes of the school is not esteemed at all. 'She keeps us in order,' said one girl in praise of a particular teacher, 'and gives us nice things to do.' And it would be no praise of a teacher to say, 'She can't keep us in order, and she gives us nothing to do.'

Within this general acceptance of measures designed to maintain order, and to establish in the pupil a degree of caution and calculation in his conduct, there remains a strong note of protest about the over-eager resort to punishment which some schools are accused of displaying. Here, our young people make a number of uncompromising demands. They ask, first, that the person-in-authority should remain a person, and recognize the personality of the pupil.

The thing teachers don't remember ... well, *they* were probably worse. This is strictly irrelevant – the doctor who advises boys not to take up smoking is not to be faulted simply because he smoked as a boy. But there may be a relevant point here. The meaning which a punishment carries depends a great deal on the quality of the personal relationship in which it is inflicted; and in the school context – and even more in the home – it carries personal overtones beyond the mere act itself. An offender in school is not being punished in the way an adult is punished in court, where impersonal criteria and the demands of justice and the safety of the community override, in the end, the feelings of the individual offender. The court is expected to take the individual situation into account, and to respect his personal rights, but it is not expected to establish a personal relationship with him. If the punishment is broadly just, therefore, it does not matter very much whether the judge is rough or gentle with the defendant; and it would certainly not help the situation if the judge confessed that he had endorsements on his licence too.

Nor, of course, would it really help in the school situation if a teacher administering punishment paused to rest his arm, and chatted nostalgically about the days when he too 'did things'. He has, after all, presumably, given them up now: and he is now supporting a rule-system that applies to him as much as to the offender.

Nevertheless, the boy who complained that teachers don't remember is feeling after a need for the recognition, in the situation, of common humanity; a recognition that school offences are failures in learning, and not to be treated in the same way as deliberate evil. It is one of the fearsome aspects of the teacher's position that he is at once victim of the offence, witness, judge and prison officer; and our young protester is here arguing for the control of this absolute power by an awareness of the bond of humanity. In simple terms, he is saying, 'Well, punish me if you must, but before you do try to put yourself in my shoes.'

The second thing they ask for is explanation:

> Punishment is useless without a talk or something afterwards ...

> If someone beening punished for something they done wrong its do them good if you tell them what right what is wrong ...

With this we should want to agree, subject to questions we might ask about the evidence for the case that 'its do them good' at all.

What is open to more controversy is the widespread claim they make that explanation and reasoning, if properly offered, will make punishment unnecessary. The boy who said he continued to smoke when his father said 'If I ever catch you I'll tan your arse', but thinks he might have given up if his father had 'explained the dangers and *advised* him not to' is perhaps over-naive. But others are not so naive. One boy spoke from the opposite experience, of having learnt from *not* being punished:

> The headmaster he didnt give me any punishment at all, he just talked to me. And I found it's a lot better and I respected him more and I still like him. Praps if he'd punished me I might not have liked him so much now.

With this cautious assessment there can surely be no disagreement.

The point at issue, indeed, is not whether reasoning can make punishment unnecessary, as the high vote for 'some children need punishment' shows; but whether punishment has any point if it is administered *without* reasoning. It is tempting to say – as so many of our young people would want us to say – that it never has, but this would be to ignore the chaotic realities of the school situation. There are certain routines – such as punctuality, reasonable quiet, appropriate dress, and the like – which need explanation when they are initiated, but which it would be tedious and naive to explain again at every infringement. It might even be said to be insulting to explain them. Most of the time children know what they are doing, and they have a tiresome need to try something on from time to time, by way of discovering where they are, and if the teacher is there too, and whether the rule-system still stands. At such moments, a teacher who laboriously explained the moral theory behind the prescription of punctuality would soon cease to be respected, in any sense of that ambiguous word. These situations are, indeed, no more than games, which would be spoilt if they became too earnest; and punishments are no more than penalty kicks, and part of the fun.

Even when the issues are more serious, it can be argued that an impersonal, unexplained enforcement of the rules can be regarded as educative. In teaching a subject, the teacher inevitably, and rightly, says from time to time, 'I can't explain that now – you'll have to take my word for it; and we'll come back to it later.' The enforcement of moral rules, in the same way, will sometimes call for the exercise of mere authority, on the ground that certain moral issues are too complex for examination at this moment. What is really being said, if this is done, is, 'You cannot learn everything at once: today's lesson is about A and B, but not about P and Q.'

But of course it is necessary to be honest about it, and to be true in purpose. The teacher who punishes without having thought about it, and without having decided that the issue really is too complex for immediate treatment, will soon be seen through by the cool, penetrating eye of childhood. It may not always be the case that

> if they are talked to, and asked why they did the thing they did,
> and you understand, They will try not to do it again,

but it really is the case that if children come to trust the situation, and can count on being listened to and reasoned with, 'it *is* ten times more effective', even if the 'reasoning' is conducted with some asperity.

The point here is simply an educational one: that learning does not progress very well if it proceeds only in general terms. The laws of science come alive when they are seen at work on a single case, when 'chemistry' is seen to be happening in the world and not only in the text-book; and an event is seen to have its reasons. And the laws of morality come alive when an unexpected moral event occurs, and the teacher stops to explore it. The truth of the matter lies in a tension between two sides of a paradox: that the enforcement of a rule will always arouse some hostility, but that if a rule is never enforced it will disappear. It is true that if the teacher shows you up and says its awful, you'd think Oh blow 'er.

But it is also true that

if I didn't get punished I would just be a spoiled brat.

Our children are aware of the tension, and are prepared to live with it.

Religious and moral education   The assumption that religious education is the vehicle of moral education dug so deep into our national ideology that the attempt to distinguish them meets with bewilderment on all sides. Simple folk, who have no time for 'all this dogma', would use the word religion as a hurrah-word, but mean by it a

sense of moral values ... Christianity is morals ... Christ was a person, giving the best example of how to live; one could not expect to be able to live like that today; still the example is there. They like to speak of 'practical Christianity' ...[7]

Many Christians, who would regard this as a highly inadequate account of Christianity, would yet be anxious about the suggestion that morality could be sustained without Christianity; and they would talk of the Christian ethic as the basis of our law and morals, and the divine moral imperative as support for standards of behaviour. Morality without religion, they would say, must become a tactic of expediency, at the mercy of changes in taste, until in the end there are no standards at all.

Most of our boys and girls will have none of all this.

I just stare out of the window and wish for the time to go by ... I mean if a bloke wants to be a teacher of religious education, then let him be that. I'm not interested in it ... I find the lessons boring. Being taught RE in school has turned me more against being religious.

And though there is usually *somebody* present to defend even Bible-teaching, which they regard as the supreme irrelevance ('I enjoyed RE – probably because of a marvellous teacher ...'), even here it is acknowledged that it can easily go astray:

Unless there is a modern, likeable and knowledgeable teacher for such a controversial subject there are bound to be problems misunderstandings and resentments.

The overriding difficulty is the Bible ('what happened in the days of Moses ect', 'pesecusion of the Christians', 'all this bible and stuff is a load of ROT').

The first difficulty is one of basic language – not merely the difficulty of the Jacobean English, which the flood of modern versions tries, but in vain, to solve; but the difficulty presented by a framework of cultural concepts which have to be learnt before they can be put to work. Before a child can grasp what the Bible is all about, he has to enter, with mind and feeling, a totally different culture. He has to perceive the relativity of the complex set of messages to a complex situation; and to pick his way, the son of a technological age, through the poetry and poetic history of a time when myth, magic and fact were inextricably mixed. Until he has achieved all this, the Bible is a very dangerous book indeed; and is in any case a very difficult book.

Now children, like the rest of us, will tackle patiently and eagerly enormous difficulties, provided they believe them to be worth the effort. They will learn a language if they first believe it means something; and to believe this, they must first find that it means something to *them*. And this is precisely what they do not find.

It is not that religion is of no interest to them. The girl who dismissed her teacher as boring because 'she reads out of the bible for hours' went on, curiously it may seem, to say

> If she'd talk about something actually dealing with our lives, you know, about religion and things ...

If we wanted to pounce on her here, we could, of course, pounce, and tie her in knots; but it would be a barren victory, for she is right, that her generation has not grasped, and is not prepared to make the effort to grasp, what it is that traditional religious language is doing. They want to talk about religion ('It's a very interesting subject – it's a very controversial subject'), but they demand that the whole matter should be dealt with in thought-forms they can already handle. They are, to put it crudely, 'Robinson-men'. Alasdair MacIntyre, in a review of *Honest to God*,[8] observed

> It is just not true that children in this country are indoctrinated in Christianity as a result of the 1944 Education Act. What they *are* indoctrinated in is confusion ... Since teachers usually do not even attempt to give any criteria for accepting or rejecting belief, many children naturally remain in a half-light between acceptance and rejection ... The secondary modern school-children of whom Harold Loukes wrote in *Teenage Religion* would suggest, for ex-

ample, that the question of whether God did or did not make the world could not be answered because nobody else can have been there to see. If they do believe in God, it is often the God 'up there' (literally, physically up) whom Dr Robinson thinks has been incredible for a long time.[9]

The sheer confusion we can see in the muddle over the Christian conscience, and guilt and forgiveness.

A good person who isn't a Christian is a better person because a Christian does something and knows it is wrong ... but somebody who doesn't know about being a Christian doesn't know any better.

Oh no, says someone else:

The Christian, soon as they do something wrong, they think that they're forgiven for it, by God, so they think that whatever they do wrong they're forgiven.

But that's not it either:

A good Christian isn't the same as a good person because they follow the ten commandments and then they look down on anybody else, look down their noses at them.

And so they give up the effort to sort it out:

Well, God's just the same as a ghost or a fairy ... Everybody has some fancy that they believe in ... Like a comic or something like that.

And they want to come to grips with the moral situation without the intrusion of the biblical machinery:

No I don't believe in the Bible and so don't get guidance from it. My parents are pretty good – so I don't need a myth to grow up straight ... my mum does not oppose church, but does not really believe in God. Yet she is the best kindest most loving woman I know.

When we ask them to consider the Christian moral ideal without the myth, they make two points of moment. First, they say, it is too far above the realities of the moral situation to be of any service.

Loving thy neighbour, it's lovely that you should strive for it, it's very nice, very good sort of thing. But it's very difficult. I think it's rather difficult for people to relate it to themselves, because it's so good.

Here, of course, there is a simple linguistic difficulty, arising from the slippery word 'love' – as, indeed, one of them pointed out, when she said 'loving as yourself' didn't mean *liking*:

> You dislike yourself. You dislike your enemy ... You've got to try and treat them as you would treat yourself in that situation.

This analysis was greeted with warm approval; but there still remains the problem that to use the language of Christian perfection as a teaching device is an educational oddity. Learning begins where the learner is, and rests on experience, not on dreams. A child does not learn to love poetry by dreaming about the perfect poem, but by reading real poems; and he learns to love goodness by seeing real goodness. But there is no entity recognizable as 'real' goodness: there are only people, acting in certain ways; and none of them is 'really' good.

> There are so many people ... that think of themselves as Christians, they go round and say they're Christians. But how many people actually do Christian things? I mean, they don't *do* anything.

This problem of the unrealized, and unrealizable, ideal comes home to them most deeply when they see it as a threat to their own identity.

> One thing they do is read a part of the bible and then try to form you into that person they're talking about.

Here we are faced by a difficulty more obstinate than the language and thought-forms of religion, and more subtle than the apparent gap between Christian aspiration and Christian reality; the difficulty that even if our children do listen to our lessons, they do not like what they hear. The perfection – the incredible perfection – of Jesus is seen as a threat to their acceptance of their own imperfect nature. Here is teacher, they say, thinking I ought to be like that; but I'm not like that; so teacher isn't on the side of the 'I' that I really am. The presentation of Jesus as a moral exemplar, to full-blooded youngsters who could not behave like him if they tried, and if they could would be laughed at and trampled on, is an exercise bound to fail. It is an attempt to sell a uniform, to train the sinews of the heart in unnatural skills, to put a mask on those eager faces full of love and hate, joy and gloom, anger and delight. But however lovely the mask, our young folk will have none of it: they need a welcome to the bare faces they have grown for themselves.

It is no defence to say, as a Christian would say, that there is no intention to present Jesus as an example for imitation, in any merely external sense; to claim that the Christian experience is not one of imitation, but of the movement of love, and that Jesus is for loving, not copying. This is true, but it is no defence; for the meaning of any teaching is the meaning the learner perceives, not the meaning the teacher intends. And what our children perceive, and I suspect must perceive, is that they are being asked to become copies and not persons.

> I know we are supposed to be like God etc but it is terribly difficult not to do wrong things, we do learn slowly but surely by our own mistakes and this is the best way. I suppose it is good to have such a shining example, but ...

The overall tone of the conversations and their individual comments conveys an impression of people who have joined the human race, in touch with the springs of human community; who have acquired some knowledge and skill, and see the need to acquire more if they are to move through the world in confidence – wanting 'to learn maths and English and all that'; but ready to do battle for the personal reality they sense in themselves – 'I don't know what they want me to be, but they can't make me other than I am.' How far they have really gone in the discovery of the reality of other persons and the imaginative entry into another's situation we cannot say. But they want to: 'personally I would rather do love, marriage, friendship, etc rather than the Bible and the Commandments, as those are necessary for a good life and happiness, and we should be taught as much as possible about them.'

It is hard to say that they are wrong.

8

The Form of Moral Education

It is tempting, in conclusion, to pontificate about a programme for moral education: to lay down a new law on the matter, to prescribe a curriculum of study, and to set up standards of achievement by which a school can measure its success. This temptation I propose to resist, for three reasons. First, the *objective* of moral education is the engagement of our children in personal living, and the criteria of success are personal and not public. Second, *any* educational programme is inescapably moral, so that when we talk about moral education we are simply talking about education in a particular way. And lastly, the drift of my argument hitherto has been that the moral education of our children, in school and home, certainly cannot be dismissed as totally ineffective.

The objectives of moral education Our point of departure must be that we cannot define moral education in terms of conformity to a particular moral code, or measure it by 'correct' responses to specific moral questions. We have become aware, thanks to the anthropologists, sociologists and to the ease of travel and communications, of the multitudinous variety of moral codes actually existing in different societees. Some of these may be 'better' or 'worse' than others, but we are becoming shy of making such judgments because we find them too complex. Sometimes a whole society is judged to be going astray (and Hitler's Germany is a great standby here) but even then, when we look at the whole way of life, we find within it human qualities we cannot simply dismiss as evil. Equally we should shrink from describing any society actually existing in the world as good enough to be conformed to. Puritan England, it is fair to say, was less licentious than Charles II's England: but if everybody had conformed, would it have been a place in which persons grew to their full stature? Should we not then have been joining that group of our boys and girls, who plead for spontaneity, arguing that goodness involves some degree of 'doing something people are happy doing, not something they didn't want to, trying and experimenting and learning from one's mistakes'?

Indeed, we should want to say that training in conformity is not to be described as education at all. We should not describe as historically educated people who repeat elegantly the Whig view of history or the Marxist view of history, or whatever orthodoxy was chosen for their acceptance: we should want them to choose among the orthodoxies, and take up a personal stance according to their own perspective on the evidence: to 'try and experiment and learn from mistakes'. But to agree on this does not answer the *educational* question, of how we develop a personal stance.

The same pattern of argument could hold in moral education. Small children certainly have to obey for most of their time, as a mere matter of survival, but we can choose to continue to demand this obedience until they are mature enough to be trusted to choose wisely (or 'rightly', or as we would choose for them) or we can choose to put them increasingly in situations where they can choose for themselves, and perhaps foolishly (or 'wrongly'), making mistakes from which they learn. Nobody now argues children should *never* be allowed any freedom to make mistakes, and nobody argues that they should never be controlled in any way; but there is a dramatic range of practice in the amount and method of control and the breadth and frequency of areas of freedom. Some infants are never out of their parents' sight; some can play, or injure or drown themselves at will. Some adolescents are allowed time to themselves only when somebody knows precisely what they will be doing; others can arrange their pot-parties and petting sessions immune from interference from anyone except the police. The method of control varies between the purely authoritarian ('Do this because I say so') and the rational where the reasons for obedience are explained ('Do this because it will be better for you in the long run, or better for me, or better for Uncle Harry'). And the quality of freedom varies between neglect ('Just run away and play, will you') and positive care ('Yes, of course you can go climbing on Scafell, so long as you have your map and a rope and send me a post-card from time to time').

The difficulty that faces us if we try to judge these variations in practice is that we have no conclusive evidence that any particular mixture is much more effective than any other; and no conclusive means of proving that a particular *effect* is more desirable than any other. The lunatic extremes are easy to rule out. A baby left to itself would die: an adolescent given no scope for judgment would either be crushed or rebel. A totally uncontrolled adult would be described as a psychopath; a totally controlled adult as a puppet. But between these extremes we cannot determine precisely what mixture of obedience and autonomy we want, or if we did by what mixture of authority and freedom we could best bring it about.

In all this confusion of thought and practice, it is possible to discern a certain outline of a theory of moral growth, which in its simplest terms would go something like this. Any life in society is conducted within a tension between the self and others. The moral self is one that takes others into account in its decision-making. The moral 'others' (authority-figures, the institutions of social control) take the reality of the self (personal needs, and desires, and dignity) into account in their use of power. The morality of a society would be evaluated by the qualities of the person of which it approved and sought to promote and the morality of a self by what it approved in society, and in other persons, and showed its approval in action. The growth of a child – physical and mental – represents at its simplest, an increase in the powers of the self, a movement from a position in which he has to obey others to a position where, within limits, he may choose not to. The moral growth of a child consists in the use of this power to choose with a due regard to the reality of the 'others'.

Granted these terms we should say that there are certain clear tasks to be performed on the way from infancy to adult life, marked by changes in the self and the others, and the relationship between them. The new-born infant is completely dependent on the others, and has no choice but to obey; and the self has no existence except a tendency to depend, to suck and welcome being cared for. His moral task, at this point, is to assert a self, which he does by shouting and screaming, threshing about, or just being sick, and to develop a self that takes account of the others, which he does by obeying, and enjoying the approval that follows obedience, or by being cute, and enjoying the surprised delight that follows his cuteness. The educational task of the others is thus to impose a beneficially authoritarian regime, so that the child can enjoy obeying it, and to delight in *him*, himself in his special being. If this primary task is not accomplished, the child may still grow up, but he will grow up without any power to take others seriously, and without a consistent self, with personal purposes. We may then call him an instance of infantile regression, or a psychopath, or simply wicked. 'The wicked man', as Hobbes said, 'is but a child grown strong.' If the task is accomplished, the child has two sources of value, approving the others and appraising the self. He approves the others because they approve the self he has developed; he approves the self because it has won approval from the others. He can obey, and also *be*. The others become real to him because the self is engaged with them; the self is real because the others assert it: he can trust, because he is trusted by those whom he had no choice but to trust.

The next development is one in which the others become more numerous, and various; and the self becomes more powerful and many sided. The child meets more and more people, some of whom are to be trusted, and some distrusted. At the same time he has more of himself to deal with: more strength and skill, more opportunity and more temptation. In this situation he can err either by failing to discriminate among the others, swim with the crowd and cease to be a person, or he can retire into himself and his private conscience, and fail to relate to the others. Most adolescents have a double life in this way: conforming to certain elements in the common culture, while recoiling in self-righteous horror from others. The fortunate ones are those who find a healthy gang to adapt to, and have a healthy private world to retire to. The unfortunate ones are those who fall among thieves without a valid private world of their own. For either, there are here two tasks: to learn to adjust to the group without losing their own identity; and to discover and develop their identity, their integrity-in-variety, without losing touch with the group.

The young adult has finally to become a person-in-relation; one who can trust himself and trust others; but control the disparate elements in himself and discriminate among others; who can take the interests of others seriously and compassionately into account, while himself remaining an authentic person; who can judge others on some rational basis, on principle, and direct his own activities coherently and purposefully; who can grasp the particularity of the particular situation, but can judge it by something he sees as the right.

From this account of the way moral growth occurs, we can set out four tasks to be accomplished at different stages. First, the small child has to learn to obey, and accept and trust. Second, he has to develop a self, a personal identity, within which a moral element, a conscience, operates. Third, he has to learn to adjust to others whom he does not obey, but whose ways of behaving he shares as a declaration of common humanity. And fourthly he has to gauge, and feel, and act with rational altruism : taking others' interests as seriously into account as his own and faithfully interpreting the particular situation in the light of general principle.

I have said 'the small child has to learn to obey'; but it is also important that the adult should continue to obey. It may not be a notable moral achievement to obey the law, or an authority figure; but it is part of a mature morality to obey where obedience is right. Equally, it is part of a mature morality to conform to the customs of those around us; and, again to stick at a point of conscience simply because 'one cannot do it'. This must be recognized, because there is a common tendency to equate 'mature morality' with nothing but rational altruism practised by the morally mature individual, working everything out himself on rational principles and compassionate insight. But when we reflect on our actions, we *do* take into account the law on the matter, the custom prevalent at the time, the promptings of conscience, and the feelings, and needs and rights of the people involved. Thus, for myself, I do not shoot students who come late to my lectures, and would claim in this respect to be a morally educated man. If I were pressed to defend this degree of permissiveness, I should give four reasons. First, it is illegal, and the state would be against me; then it is simply not 'done', and the other students would laugh at me; further, I do not see myself as a shooting man – this is not my self-image; and finally, I hope, there is some touch of compassion and concern, of feeling what it is like to be late for a lecture, some awareness of fact-and-consequence (they would be dead, and unable to hear the rest of the lecture) and some of personal direction and commitment.

It is important to remind ourselves of this, to make clear that being morally educated is not to be defined *solely* in terms of working out a personal morality on the basis of one's own moral experience, or to stigmatize as immature, or amoral, any behaviour that springs from rule-keeping or social conformity, or obstinate conscience, because in practice we recognize as morally mature those people who arrive at their decisions by taking them all into account. Someone who says, 'Well, I've thought it out as faithfully as I can, but I'm still in doubt, so I will obey the law, or do what other people do, or respond to the prickings of conscience', is not to be written off as a moral infant. Indeed, we should say that an individual who confidently follows his own reasoning *without* paying serious heed to the law and the custom and his conscience is in fearsome danger of going wrong. The true conscientious objector to war is not one who jumps to the conclusion that making love is better, but one who has done battle in his soul with the imperative of the state, the anxieties of his fellows, and his own image of himself as a man of action: and still decides there is a better way to which he must be loyal.

A realistic concept of the morally educated man is thus one that describes him as having learnt obedience, conformity and conscience, together with an ability to hold them in relationship. He has learnt to judge one by the other, and has developed criteria for choosing between them. He judges the traditional code by the degree to which people actually follow it (as our boys and girls did with lying); or he judges the current custom by the vision inherited from the past (as we do when we bring contemporary life to the judgment of New Testament ethics); or he judges both by his own conscience, when he resists temptations to which he would be ashamed in his heart to yield. And in the process, he employs his concern and compassion, his understanding of the situation, and in the end stands or falls by the depth of his personal involvement.

Morality in education   My second reason for arguing that we do not need a radically new law and school subject is that moral education is not a distinctive item in the curriculum or school organization, but an aspect or quality of any education. This point would be so obvious as to be hardly worth making, were it not for the nonsense that has been talked in much of the recent debate; by those hard-pressed teachers who groaned and said 'What, all this, and now morals too?' and by the opportunists who saw a new subject here, ME, to range alongside PE and RE (or perhaps to displace RE), with qualifications for teachers, CSE options and special allowances.

Yet the point is simple. To be moral is to behave in such a way as to take other people into consideration; to be immoral is to behave without taking other persons into consideration. Any behaviour that could conceivably affect other people is therefore moral or immoral behaviour. It is difficult to see how there can be behaviour that does not potentially affect other people. Being asleep may seem tolerably neutral, but moral questions are raised by being asleep on duty, or not sleeping enough so that next day one is no use to anybody. If people behave at all, they behave morally or immorally: just as they behave efficiently or inefficiently.

Now education is a process in which some persons set out deliberately to make a change in some other persons: and it is inescapably moral or immoral. It can change them for good or for ill. If it fails altogether it fails to be good. Nothing can *be* at all without being good or bad; and no relationships can *be* without being good or bad relationships.

It can be objected that 'good', as a general term of approval, has a wider reference than 'moral'. We can talk of 'good' weather, or good food or a good garden, without finding it necessary to import moral categories; but human beings actually at work or play always act morally or immorally. The most elementary teaching situation, indeed, calls precisely for the teacher and the pupil to display compassionate concern, faithfulness to truth, and commitment and self-control. Nobody can start to teach mathematics (a morally neutral subject if there ever were one) without taking seriously the child's personal claim to learn it. Nor can the child begin to learn it unless he respects the person of the teacher, listens to him and seriously considers what he has to say, and accepts his right to say it. Nor can we teach without some inkling of what it feels like to be ignorant and puzzled, and to be corrected in a mistake; the pupil must catch from his teacher some feeling for mathematics, must be stirred in some degree by the teacher's own pleasure in this form of understanding. We cannot teach or learn without inferring general principles from particular situations, for this is what all learning is in the end about. And to teach at all the teacher must be personally committed to this task to the exclusion for the moment of all others, and must hold on to his purpose through trial and temptation; and the child must be absorbed to the point where this purpose takes hold of him, and he works, and learns, using the tool as a development of his personal identity. Teaching is, quite simply, a moral business; and it is in the *business* rather than in exhortation that the important lessons are learnt. To be treated morally is more educative than to be preached at, and to be taught *with* moral concern more educative than to be urged to *show* it. We have all seen end-of-term reports urging that 'he should learn to pay more attention', or 'he shows no interest', or 'he should learn to think', or 'he could do better if he tried harder' – all, in a way, lauding the morality of learning. But in the learning of morality, children live by what they see more than what they hear.

The case I am arguing is that moral education is not to be thought of as a new course of study, to be introduced alongside all the others, but as paying attention to the way the other subjects are presented. It is also part of my case, as I hope by now has become abundantly clear, that the schools are not to be accused of total failure in their moral responsibility. It has been said that teachers are *good* people: what else could they be, living all day in the company of such trust and hope and spontaneous warmth? Of course, like any group of people, they vary: they fail, if not to be perfect is to fail, and some are withdrawn, or aggressive, or simply tired. But it is not a profession to attract the greedy, or the cruel, or the cold, and the way our boys and girls talk suggests power-fully that they have not found it so.

Those who lay the ills of modern society at the doors of the school, forget two things: that the fundamental moral learning is acquired in the home and the intimate relationships of childhood and youth; and that the continuance of moral purpose depends on the society they live in as adults.

The school can reasonably be expected to make changes in its pupils' attitudes and ways of understanding, but it cannot make radical changes in personality or in the social structure. It is not a hospital for the mentally and morally sick; and it is not an instrument of social conditioning charged with the imprinting of moral responses guaranteed not to fade for fifty years.

The task of the school   My argument is not to be pushed to extremes: either to the position that all the school has to do is to get on with its teaching of science and art, and morality can be left to take care of itself; or that though there *is* a task to be done, it is all being done as well as it could be. All I am arguing is that the task is implicit in everything else and is per-formed through the medium of everything else; and that the task has not been totally neglected.

What, then, is the task? How can it be defined in realistic terms as a task within the powers of ordinarily good people to perform?

It may help us to get clear about it if we consider the task of the school in the conduct of any other element in education, such as the production of historically educated men. Here, too, we should say that 'relatively enduring personal characteristics' set, also say that the ripening of a historically educated person, and the degree to which he will actually behave historically, will depend before we start, limits to what we can hope to achieve. We should on his 'wider social context and group loyalties', such as whether or not he associates with other historically-minded people. But between these two limitations the school would set itself four kinds of objectives:

1. To give the pupil a broad grasp of what is going on, to initiate him into the tradition as it at present works, of what it means to 'do' history. In thus grasping the general point, the pupil is under authority: he must learn and follow the rules, copy other men's procedures, and broadly accept the established criteria of being a historian. No amount of talk about discovery methods or creativity can shake this overriding demand for acceptance. He must even accept, on authority, most of what historians say: he cannot repeat, in his school life, all the investigations that hundreds of historians have made in centuries. Even though we may, from time to time, get him to investigate, we do it in order to show him how it is done: and if he strays from the received tradition, and tries to discover if the Bayeux Tapestry will burn, we tell him, No, that is not history: that is chemistry.

2. To give the pupil a grasp of the language involved in history, and to get him to take it, along with other living historians (who are fellow learners) in such a way that he can share in the current mood, and current interests. The solitary scholar, discovering truth on a mountain top, is an imaginary figure: even Browning's Grammarian arrived there only for his funeral. The established tradition of what it means to be a historian is always subtly changing; and the young historian must be grasped by the tradition but exposed to the change.

3. To give him sufficient successful practice in the tools of the historian's task that he becomes personally identified with it, and begins to see himself as a historian. This is to develop, as it were, a historian's conscience, a habit of seeing the element of historicity in a situation as the one he is concerned with, that he deeply cares about.

4. To combine these areas of learning in insight and originality and creativeness in the solution of specific historical problems. While he is in school, these problems will be selected and limited, but they may be real problems, with no agreed solution: and he must bring to them insight into the tradition, to the working thoughts of living students, and his own involvement and concern.

If we transfer this analysis from historical education to moral education, we find ourselves talking of the application of our four moral modes, with the school's task defined as the development of understanding in all four. It is for the school to initiate into the corpus of established moral rules, to demonstrate their point, where they came from, and what they achieve; to engage the pupil in active group relations so that he understands the contemporary mood, and speaks to it; to give opportunity for the exploration, and exercise, of conscience; and to provide a base for the interaction of the other three modes in the development of moral insight and decision-making. Let us look at each in turn.

Living under rule   The small baby has no choice but to trust in the decisions of another person, and he grows, or fails to grow, according to whether or not his trust is shown to be justified; and the degree to which the other person cares, consistently and predictably, warmly, affectionately, caring for him as a person. The moral adult still needs this basic trust, but now it must be found in an infinitely wider range of relationships. He will need a few intimately personal relationships, perhaps only one, but he will also need to live in trust with hosts of people he hardly knows. Of them, he will not ask that they care especially for him, for it is as true for them as for him that 'there are so many people', and you cannot like them all. So from them he asks only for predictable respect, which he can learn about, and respect in his turn. He must know that other people will behave, tolerably consistently, according to rule, and by the overriding rule of impartiality, he must learn to live under rule himself.

It is necessary to make these obvious remarks because of the irritation with rules expressed today in dreams of an 'alternative society', or the de-schooling movement, and even some Christian language about the gospel of love as a gospel of liberation from the law. But the truth is that rules are necessary to loving, for they describe the way people expect each other to behave, and without knowing this expectation we cannot love them until we know all about them. We cannot 'do unto others' unless we know how people expect to be done by.

The school, with its cooler relationships than the home ('Teachers are strangers really') is thus not an obstacle to moral growth, replacing persons by legislation: it is a place where living under rule can be learnt; where it can be discovered that strangers can trust each other; and where the identity of the person can be developed with some degree of conscious choice and direction. The school properly differs from the home because the rules take less account of individual whimsy: they are more generalized, and call for more obedience and more accommodation from the individual. It often makes sense in the home to say that if a child does not 'feel like' doing something now, he can put it off until he does: it rarely makes sense to say the same in school. Equally it makes sense to say that in the home rules should be as few as possible, and concerned only with important matters: but school rules may be – indeed must be – manifold and complex, and often concerned with apparently trivial matters. Dick, drawing his picture at home, does not need to sign it and keep it in a folder; Richard, painting in school, will lose it if he doesn't.

School rules represent a half-way house to the adult situation of living under law, and a means of learning what it is like to do so. They resemble the law in providing the structure of community; they differ in the fact that the community is concerned with learning, and the rules are to be defined as not merely protective of the community but educative for the members. We judge them not only by their success in maintaining order, but also by their success in enabling children to learn and grow. It is round the tension between these two objectives that the argument gathers, with the voice of Summerhill pleading that growth comes only from free choice, and the voice of the tradition replying that subjugation to order is a precondition of the power to choose.

There is no way of resolving the argument in abstract terms, but only in specific situations: the particular rule and its special purpose, the particular people and their special needs. All that can be said is that to be morally educative rules should be *made* clear, as distinct from merely *being* clear (the law of the land tries to *be* clear, but nobody except a lawyer understands it); that they should be, at all relevant points, binding on all members of the community, staff as well as children; and that they should be open to examination and revision by all members of the community.

No one would question the need for clarity and explanation: rules cannot be teaching devices if they are not taught. The least formal infant class calls for a vast amount of sheer explanation, about what is done and what not done, what the apparatus is for and how it should be used. And in the least formal situation there will be children who wander beyond the bounds, and have to be recalled and instructed. Freedom to explore is splendid, but it does not include freedom to explore a motorway in full flow.

It may seem less obvious that rules should apply to staff and children alike. Staff and children are not alike: their functions are not alike: and so the rules must differ. There can be a perfectly proper rule that children go into the playground at break while the staff can stay indoors if they please. But it is still true that staff should be seen to live under rule: to be broadly consistent in their policies, to obey the necessity for punctuality, to respect the *obverse* of rules-for-learning by obeying the rules-for-teaching, to match the demand for regularity by impartiality, the demand for truth-telling by truth-telling, to be subordinated to the purpose of the community to the same degree as the children. The famous remark 'He is a beast, but a just beast' carries the first moral demand from the child on the school community: that it should work not on whim but on impartiality between persons. It would be better if he were not a beast; but then we are all a little beastly, and yet can learn justice.

More controversial is the demand that rules should be open to revision by all members of the community. In saying this, I rule out the simple imposition of rules by the hierarchy, but I also rule out abdication to pupil-power. Both forms of rule-system, drawn up by one side only, fail to be morally educative because they fail in respect for persons. Persons are not being respected if they are not permitted to say what it feels like to be the people they are in the situation they are in. In the end, the principle still holds that only the educated can settle the terms on which education is to be conducted; but on the long road before the end, the educated and the less-educated must actually hear each other about their common plight. Whether or not this hearing is done through institutions, such as a school council or a referendum, or is conducted informally, does not very much matter. A splendid school council which is regarded merely as a toy or a safety-valve is less morally educative than an infant teacher going into an honest huddle with her class about how to distribute the milk. School rules represent an essential moral code, but they come under judgment from peer-group values and from personal conscience. When we blindly make rules about personal appearance we may attack an adolescent at a vital point. A boy at a boarding school complained that when he was sent home with short hair at the end of term he was jeered by all his friends. We are entitled to insist on standards in the school, but are we morally educative if we tangle up group-relationships?

Similarly, in so far as conscience is still for the adolescent a living nexus with a home that he still trusts, the conflict between school ethics and home ethics will often be a conflict of conscience. The message of many homes – and it is not altogether a bad message – is 'You don't have to knuckle under'. Before we leap to asserting our standards, we should perhaps be tender in our common exploration of what knuckling under means, pushed to the indefinable, but not unexaminable, frontiers of the role and sources of authority, conformity and conscience.

The critical point of any rule-system is to be seen at the moment of enforcement. A rule that is not observed is not a rule: the word carries an implication of some sort of enforcement, either by unfailing supervision, suasion, bribery or deterrent penalty. Here we find ourselves today in some difficulty. Ceaseless supervision seems a poor means of creating trust. Suasion and bribery may control behaviour, but at the cost of displacement of motive, substituting the pleasing-teacher syndrome or pure greed for moral insight. And punishment looks at first sight a simple denial of personal relationships. Our boys and girls, giving punishment their first sight, plead that it should be replaced by a 'good talking to' – though on second thoughts, some admit that they have learned from being punished themselves, and the majority, reluctantly, that 'You have to have it – some people need punishment'. But who needs it? And how do we know when to give it?

The situation is too complex for glib pronouncements. All that can be said is that the decision to punish or not to punish is a moral decision, to be taken in a moral mode and not merely an administrative mode. The teacher must take into account respect for persons, *this* person and all the other persons, the feelings of the persons, the consequences of the punishment, the general principle implicit in it, and his own responsibility. If he conceives the situation too narrowly, in terms of his face-to-face relations with the individual offender, he may be too 'soft', judging that the person-here and his feelings now, and the consequence in his attitude ('It makes you hate the teacher') call for overlooking the offence. If he conceives it too widely, in terms of public order, he may be too 'hard', judging that deterrence of others, or of this individual-in-the-future, and the consequences in relative peace call for instant suppression. Two contradictory facts in the experience of teachers are inescapable: that children often find school boring, and exploit the 'soft' teacher as an opportunity for some excitement; and that teachers who have established their position as initiators of work soon find that the need for punishment rarely arises. Somewhere between these conflicting facts lies a line of development in the enforcement of a code of behaviour.

There seem to be no facts hard enough to get hold of in the

problem of what sanctions to use, such as choosing or rejecting corporal punishment. There is an abundance of opinion, and an increasing readiness among heads to declare to the school, that the cane has been abolished with, it is reported, consequent improvement in personal relationships. The difficulty in handling such evidence is that we cannot isolate the simple decision on the cane from the multitude of other decisions an abolitionist is likely to make. Such a person presumably values relationships more than a cane-happy flogger, so he pays more attention to them.

Our young folk, if they were asked their views on this question, would probably say that though it was necessary it must not be regarded as the *last* resort so much as an item in a process of reasoning. It might be defensible for a teacher to say, 'Well, I'm going to punish you now, and then we must spend some time finding how to help you.' It is indefensible for him to say, 'You've had plenty of warning: the only thing left is the stick.' For after the stick there is a good deal left.

Living with other people   When we talk of living with other people we are talking about the inevitable, which is not susceptible to much direction or control. They just *do* it, these boys and girls, and they learn from it; just as we all do it, and learn from it. Furthermore, they, like the rest of us, live with different groups of people, with whom they behave in different ways, and from whom they learn different moral lessons; and apart from occasional attempts to forbid them to join Hell's Angels or go to a teenage petting party, there is not much we can do about it. This dimension in moral education is therefore largely beyond our control, either to promote or to reduce. Tough parents may hope to protect their children from the worst dangers, but some risk is not merely inevitable, but desirable. Learning to live with different groups is necessary to the establishment of identity. We may, in our social engineering, organize a multitude of youth-groups to promote acceptable values, but we cannot make boys and girls join them. Nor, if we could, can such groups be guaranteed to have personal significance for their members.

It has recently become fashionable to argue, however, that our rapidly-growing knowledge of group-dynamics could be profitably applied to school life. Here, the argument runs, we have a permanent society within which group-structures will develop, and may be open in a measure to our manipulation. Is it not time, then, that all teachers should be equipped in the application of group-theory, so that they can manipulate to some effect?

It is not at all clear, however, that group-theory offers a very illuminating model for what actually goes on in school. Its relevance to education lies only in the analysis of *significant* groups, groups which offer to their members experience of basic trust, support for their own identity and a sense of mutual relationship. The criteria of such a group would be:

1. The presence of face-to-face relationships and a sense of common membership.

2. The acceptance of common goals, which generate an appropriate set of norms and standards of behaviour.

3. The development within the group of different roles appropriate to different persons. A significant group thus has its leaders and its led, and among the led, differences in the ways in which they respond to leadership and to each other.

To some degree, a healthy school tries to meet these criteria: it engages in group-work, to replace the teacher-pupil dependency by pupil interdependence; it seeks to engage interest in the common goal of learning, and establish behaviour appropriate to learning; and it accepts the fact that children will differ in their responses. But the stubborn fact remains that children did not choose to come to school: they did not choose the learning goal, and if left to themselves would not want to be quiet and concentrate on a piece of work until they have finished it; and though personal differences emerge in the learning process, they fall short of group-expectations. The clever child is not a leader, and the slow child is not led.

The truth is that group-theory is appropriate in the classroom only to friendship groups, arising spontaneously within it. We could, if we wished, manipulate these to some extent, by careful planning of seating arrangements (pupils who sit at the end of rows have less friends than those who sit in the middle) and by subtle rewards for certain forms of leadership. But it would be a dangerous exercise, and would call for more skill than we can at present claim.

It could be objected in any case that it would be an immoral exercise. A child's trust would be weakened, not strengthened, by an attack on his choice of friends; his identity weakened, and the development of real relationships handicapped. It would be, at a radical level, a denial of respect for persons, both the person we hope to protect and the person we hope to protect him from.

Three points, however, do call for attention in the light of our understanding of group structures. The first is concerned with streaming itself. When we create A streams we also create C streams. We therefore create places in which the majority values will be opposed to the values we set out to promote, and in which personal identity is hard to achieve. More subtly harmful, we create A streams in which identity is not extended by variety and conflict, and in which children cannot feel in anticipation the pressures that will exert themselves later. And though the learning task will call for some kind of organization hostile to spontaneous groups, there must be continuous scrutiny of such structures in the light of group theory.

Second, the school needs to promote a rich variety of interest-groups, within which children can pursue their own goals, deal with each other and make their plans together, and throw up their own leaders. A school taking moral education seriously will be marked by its multitude of extra-curricular societies, both those dependent on the curriculum itself (like the Natural History Society, Debating Society and Music Club) and those springing from lively, current, and perhaps short-lived interests. Here we engage school goals with the purpose of its members; the teacher becomes in some sense a participant with a different, more personal role; and the members learn to use each others language in the discussion of what they judge of value.

Finally, we should ask how far the teacher, encountering a class, needs to apply concepts of group structure to his management of the situation. On this issue, Hargreaves asks whether teachers need new courses in group dynamics, and answers, irresistibly:

> We do not merely want to provide teachers with the *intellectual* knowledge and skill to ask questions. We are, presumably, aiming beyond this, towards *sensitizing* teachers to *recognizing* the problems and towards providing them with methods by which they can also *answer* the questions and *apply* what they know ... I am sceptical that a knowledge of group dynamics will in itself sensitize a teacher to the group dynamics of a classroom. Some teachers do have a 'natural' understanding of classroom group dynamics, though they cannot usually couch their understanding in technical language. Training in group dynamics might help them to conceptualize their 'natural' knowledge, but it might have the reverse effect, as in the proverbial case of the centipede and his legs.[10]

In support of his case, Hargreaves advances the notion of a Sociological Myth, whereby teachers become so learned on the influence of home environment that they lower their expectations of deprived children, and in consequence make the myth come true. Similarly, we might labour so skilfully to produce the ideal group that we destroy the reality. What matters in our children's group-life is not that our myths should come true, but that they should explore the truth within their own.

What the school *can* do is to help the children understand. If it be accepted that the most significant teaching consists of the analysis of experience, then boys and girls should engage in the analysis of *this* experience, of the living in an assortment of groups, facing the conflict of loyalties to a friend, and different friends, different groups, and in the end to abstract right and wrong. Our young folk were powerfully drawn to putting personal loyalty first, and were only just beginning to see that loyalty to right might work for the good of persons. From this beginning they need help in proceeding. Beyond the mere tug of the personal and the general lies the possibility of judging the values obtaining in different groups, and the degree to which they are indeed personal, and not merely institutional. In such a discussion the object would not be sophistication in group dynamics, but consciousness of pressures that they must learn both to resist and to welcome: to resist when they threaten their identity, and to welcome as a means of developing identity-in-relation.

Living with conscience The notion of conscience has had a chequered history in recent years. It is sometimes represented as a largely irrational, sub-conscious super-ego, resulting from early relationships with parents, and pursuing the self with a fearsome armoury of inhibition and guilt, and so is always suspect. At others it is a supra-rational revelation of categorical moral imperative, or the will of God for the person, and always to be trusted. As a word for general currency, it has become too slippery for easy use. If it is merely a parental bequest, then it will be thought something of an embarrassment; if it is an irruption of cosmic value, transcending the chaos of moral pressures in which we live, then it is a light for our guidance, and we shall want to seek it.

The concept receives little attention in educational theory for the simple reason that the school presents no acute problems of conscience in any sense of the word. It is difficult to see how anyone could claim a conscientious objection to education as such; and when the C stream import their self-image as fun-seekers, then by the criteria of education such notions must be judged at the least to be temporarily inappropriate. Further, the individual conscience is so private an affair, so compounded of attitudes derived from forgotten experiences, so variously penetrated with images of mother's smiles and frowns, and the turn of a paternal eyebrow, that it is difficult to see what any kind of public instruction can have to do with it.

Yet it remains important, and calls for our attention. The reality of relationships turns on a subtle appraisal of the other person's approval, and the way in which the first discovery of approval was made affects our responses inexorably throughout life: it is the medium of learning respect for persons; and the mechanism of inhibition and guilt is essential, to the end, as a stabilizing factor in personal conduct. It is the ultimate deterrent, when other deterrents are forgotten; it is the source of the control and direction of impulse. It is always at the centre of the storm, when wind and tide are in conflict. When George Fox said, 'Christ saith this, the apostles say this; what canst thou say?', he set his followers on the path to the exploration of conscience.

What would it mean to advance the proposition that the school is a place for 'the exploration of conscience'? It would mean certainly – and this we would say is generally the case – that the authority structure is efficient enough to protect children from any serious crisis of conscience under pressure from their peers. Most schools would justifiably claim that in this they are successful: children do not go in fear of blackmail, or pressure to join a young mafia. A little insolence, a little bullying, copying another's work, some mild pornography – there is not much of consequence a child can do. And this broadly protective structure is to be defended, on grounds of conscience, against the illusion that if children are 'trusted', they will respond to trust. True, trust breeds trust, but the maintenance of a broadly watchful control creates a *situation* to be trusted, and protects the immature conscience from exploitation.

At the same time, the school has a dangerous power, as it performs its proper task, to assault a child's image of himself as an agent, still supported by home ties. I have already instanced the problem of the hair-cut, but the matter is more complex than that. When we correct a child's English, we attack the language he has learnt at home; when we set the school ethic against the standards of the C stream, we may strike deeper; and when we try to teach an alien religion, whether more rational than that of a narrow sect or more religious than that of an atheist home, we may be attacking a child's image of himself as the child of his parents. 'Teachers are strangers really'; and strangers are wise to avoid the question, 'Are you saved?'

Now of course all these things must be done: education is about the initiation into the public and appropriate forms of discourse and understanding and behaviour; and the decision to set up a public system of education was precisely a decision to interfere in public with private conscience. But it must be done tenderly and appropriately, and with respect for persons. A surgeon, faced by the lamentable position in which he has to assault a person's body, yet performs tenderly and appropriately, and with respect to the tissue on which he works. The theatre of the school is one in which it is only too easy to work with a kind of ruthlessness, and to convey the impression that 'teachers don't care really'.

This tender respect for conscience as a child's personal roots in the home needs to be held in tension with his journey into the future: he does not *belong* to his parents, any more than he belongs to teachers. The school has the task of enlarging the conscience, of engaging it in learning, and extending its field of reference. Much of the psychological work on conscience has been concerned with the way we all vary from situation to situation, being honest in one and at least slipshod in another. The school is a place for meeting new situations and new forms of personal being, and thus learning to see oneself consistently personal in all of them: as an honest scientist, or an honest reader of books, trying in all the manifold learning roles to appraise the evidence and arrive at the right answer. When we talk of teaching from interest we are really committed to the development of conscience, by finding, within the public form of thought, something in which the person will find value and importance to his own purposes, and so to open up the holy ground on which persons traffic with each other. To teach from interest is to teach from conscience.

Religious and moral education Finally, what are we to make of the widespread hostility to religious education, the charge that it is boring and irrelevant, that Christians talk too much about God and don't *do* anything, and that even the attractiveness of the Christian ideal, at its loveliest, is so impossible to achieve that it is an obstacle and no help in the actual process of living? Can we meet this only by creating a new 'subject' called 'ME' with a new teaching force of experts in goodness? It seems an alarming conclusion to reach: are we really compelled to reach it?

The arguments in favour are serious arguments. It is clear that the present generation is not prepared to grapple with religious language sufficiently to make moral (or indeed any) sense of it. Making sense of it, we must remember, demands an enormous effort of historical imagination, cultural transfer, abstract thought and subtle casuistry, to a degree unattainable by any but a few. To use the Bible as a text-book of morality is a near-impossibility; to misuse it, a perilous exercise; and to talk glibly about the will of God, without complex examination of the actual moral situation, and a long and devoted exploration of the concept of God, is to darken counsel, not illuminate it. This is no sudden failure of the modern mind: it has always been so. Jesus spent much of his time attacking the Scribes and Pharisees for their misuse of scripture, and seeking to substitute the law of the person for the law of the book. And in the development of Christian behaviour the Bible has always been a dangerous book unless it has been subject to the judgment of living experience and authoritative interpretation. Even the early Puritans, who chose it as their final authority against the authority of the Pope, used it for the most part as an element in the authority of the congregation. It was never, and by its nature could never be, morally prescriptive: it could not, and cannot, 'tell you what to do'. At best it was holy ground between persons who were committed to loving and caring; at worst, a device for defending what one wanted to do on other grounds. At both best and worst it was the medium of communication about what was learnt in actual living, whether love-in-worship and caring-in-fellowship, or the ruthless following of the individual will. Its value for moral learning and as a vehicle of moral hope lay in the relationships of those who used it: in the degree to which they took each other seriously, and listened to their interpretations of their personal experience – whether under authority, as in the confessional or the moral sermon, or in the sharing of the moral struggle in daily life. They found religious language illuminating and helpful because they shared a common experience of worship and commitment to fellowship.

This common experience and commitment is not at present available to our children. We may wish it were, but we cannot pretend to ourselves that it is. They do not, in reality, hear people working out their personal situation in religious language, and they are not, most of them, members of a close-knit Christian fellowship exploring together the tensions of daily life. In such a situation the Bible becomes an alien document associated with unacceptable authority ('It shouldn't be a commandment ...') and suspected of threatening personal growth ('They read to you about a character in the bible and try to make you like him').

Beneath this difficulty lies a deeper one, embedded in the logic of moral and religious language. If we are to use the concept of God as a basis for concepts of goodness, we must first establish that we understand 'God' better than we understand 'goodness'. This is plainly untrue of our boys and girls: the rich content they gave to 'goodness' is different altogether from the muddle they are in over 'God'. Further, and this holds for us all, the logic of the statement 'God is good' pre-supposes that *some* meaning is already attached to 'good'. Our children are logically right, then, and deserve to be listened to, when they ask for talk about goodness before talk about God; and the argument now being pressed for a divorce between religious and moral education has much force.

Yet Christians remain a little uneasy, and cannot so lightly deny their own experience. They would agree with much of the argument, admitting that the institutions of religion – church and priest, scripture and ethical prescription – have lost their authority over all but their own adherents, and over many of *them*. They would agree that situation ethics and personal differences search out the general moral rules. They would agree that the ideal of love is rarely seen in practice. And of the religious quest itself they would say that godliness is not simply a means to the improvement of conduct: God is not a probation-officer, to be called into maintain the moral law.

Yet they would stick at the proposition that religion and ethics can be finally distinguished. Religion is concerned with the way things are: how they are now, and how they *ultimately* are; and so with the relationship between 'are now' and 'ultimately are'; and with a moral 'ought to be'. The religious experience is an inescapably ethical experience: of a strange nudge towards another sort of being, experienced in worship, or discovering possibilities of being in fellowship; of plumbing personal being in meditation, down to a level of identity beneath the conflict of role and the impulse of the moment. As they reflect on all this Christians fear a moral education cut off from these deep roots: training in the authoritative ideology, exposure to contemporary custom, decisions arrived at in a situation so narrowly conceived that the ultimate hope is denied.

But our children do not want us to do this. They have their own hopes, and sense of mystery and deep tenderness, and they are ready to traffic with ours. They ask us simply not to be irrelevant to their personal situation: to face the fact that they are already alive in a world of moral choice, and need to be listened to as they examine it for themselves. They ask nothing more of us than to 'begin here' instead of beginning 'out there'. It is not much to ask: it is not even a new thing to ask; and it is in any case no more than the demand that religious education and moral education should be genuinely educational.

When we do begin here, the elements of experience are common to both sorts of inquiry. When we use moral words like compassion and concern, altruism and insight, we use language that is at least potentially religious. Similarly, the moral concepts of the medieval church (the four cardinal virtues, for example, of prudence, justice, temperance and fortitude) are still worth exploring. The moral frontier is always potentially a religious frontier. When we have made our skilful analysis of a moral dilemma, and have arrived at a logically impeccable answer to the question, 'What ought I to do?' the further question still remains, 'But why should I do it?' True, it is illogical to ask it: we certainly ought to do what we ought to do; but then, why should we not behave in an illogical manner?

At this point it is not enough to give reasons, or even to *see* reasons: one has to sense oneself as belonging to the reasons, as being, in one's deepest identity, a part of the way things are: and in the exploration of this level of being religious language is still more helpful than any other. The language of definition, precision, and argumentation is essential in clearing the ground of moral decision: to live on that ground may call for a language of disclosure, evocation and distant hope.

If we concede this case, that the moral world pushes to the frontier of the human world, and that the question 'Why be a good human being?' does not stop until it is touching the question 'Why be human at all?', then we may also concede in so far as they are 'subjects' for study, 'RE' and 'ME' may be conducted by the same teachers. They need not be people of particular religious orthodoxy or learned in the history of ethics, so long as they are interested in, and enjoy, the kind of moral discourse I have reported, can be 'sympathetic listeners', to catch and respect the eager note of concern characteristic of young folk, and have themselves preserved hope, and are not retiring behind a defensive line of moral certitude. The name they choose to give their subject is no great matter, so long as it does not promise more than it can perform. The great matter lies in the extent to which the conversation is conducted in trust and respect and relationship and concern with the being of persons, the way it 'comes home to men's business and bosoms'.

Where, it may be, our young folk must finally be listened to is in the claim that moral questions must first be examined as moral questions and not as religious questions. They have their own vision of goodness, and they want to explore it and search it out, to see if it really works in their daily going about the world. They ask for realism, not the false realism of the cynic, which they know – perhaps more surely than we do – to be false; but the realism of an honest look at the facts of the case and the consequences of action. They ask for rationality, for the examination of reasons; and if they seem often to be complaining about the unreasonableness of *our* rules, they are still asking for reasons, which are better things to ask for than rules. And in this insistent probing, it may be said that they are more moral than those who simply lay down the law and the prophets.

Appendix

The Questionnaire

Schools and teachers think of themselves as helping you to do two things. One is to learn English and maths and so on, so that you can earn a living and understand the world. The other is to help you to grow up as a good person.

This paper asks you to say something about how you respond to the second of these.

The paper consists of remarks made in discussion by boys and girls of your own age: and you are asked to say whether you agree or not, and why; and to say anything else you would like to.

You are not asked to put your name on the paper.　But, please say

　　　　　　　　　　　　　Boy or girl?　........
　　　　　　　　　　　　　Age　　　........

Nobody will identify you.
So please be as candid as you can.

Don't think it is a waste of time. One of the ways schools can be made better is by asking boys and girls what they think; and what you say will be taken seriously.

Thank you for helping us.

1　THE PROBLEM OF RIGHT AND WRONG

(*a*)　*Always wrong*

Is there any sort of action you would want to say was always wrong?

Killing somebody　　　　　　　　　　　　A ☐

But somebody you kill might have killed your
wife or somebody. Then it's not so wrong to kill
them back.　　　　　　　　　　　　　　　B ☐

Tick the answer you prefer.

Can you think of up to five things you would say were always wrong?

(b) *Lying*

Would you say that lying is always wrong?

> No.

Then what do you say about it?

> Well, there's a lie that doesn't really matter. There's little lies and big lies. Little lies are just fibs.

> You're protecting a friend, say, that's just a fib; and there's *lies* when you're protecting yourself.

> No there's small fibs to protect yourself. I mean you took an apple off a tree and you say you never took it. I mean there's nothing wrong with that is there? But as soon as you say somebody else took it, it's a big lie.

Do you think lying is	Never wrong	A ☐
	Sometimes wrong	B ☐
	Always wrong	C ☐

Tick the answer you prefer.

Why?

(c) *Shoplifting*

What about shoplifting? Is it wrong?

> No, might not be. If you're starving to death, then nicking to stay alive is OK.   A ☐

> Once you start taking things you're gonna build up to be a big criminal.   B ☐

> It's depriving other people of their property. If you were the person who owned it you'd think of it in a different way.   C ☐

Tick the statement you prefer.

Would *you* want to say that some sorts of shoplifting are right?

2 MERCY-KILLING

(a) *The old*

Do you think people with an incurable and painful disease should be put to death?

> It's up to the person concerned.

Well, if the person concerned says to the doctor, Look, for heaven's sake, finish me off today?

> No that would be killing people. A ☐

> If he asked the doctor to kill him that would be committing suicide. B ☐

> But if you want to die you can die. It's up to you. It's no one else's life. They can't keep you alive if you want to die. C ☐

Tick the one you prefer.

(b) *A handicapped baby*

If a baby arrives, and it's terribly badly handicapped, would you kill it?

> They should say to the parents, I can't do anything about it; then the parents can decide.

> A baby was born once, and the doctor said, If the mother sees the baby it'll shock her so she'll never be the same again. So he killed it.

And you approve of this?

> I don't know.

Would you   approve of killing a handicapped baby?   A ☐

            disapprove?   B ☐

            not know?   C ☐

Have you anything else to say about either of these cases?

3 DRUGS

Do you think we ought to make cannabis legal?

> No, I say hash and pot and things should be forbidden.

And you don't mind not being able to buy it yourselves?

What would I want to buy it for? We know
what's happened to other people, so why should
we want to buy it?   A ☐

I think taking drugs is all right as long as you
don't try to persuade someone else to take them.   B ☐

What right have the police to stop you taking
drugs?   C ☐

Tick the statement you prefer.

Have you anything else to say?

4   A GOOD PERSON

This piece comes from a discussion in a classroom. The teacher
asked:

What sort of a person would you describe as a 'good person'?

Somebody doing something they were happy
doing, that they were good at, not doing something they didn't want to.   A ☐

Somebody who tries to change things and make
them better, to make less poverty and make it
easier for people to live.   B ☐

Somebody who has a posh car, nice wife, doesn't
go to Bingo, and you never hear him swear.   C ☐

No, that's a goody goody. A good man in my
mind is a man who tries everything and experiments with living and learns by his own
mistakes.   D ☐

Somebody who can listen sympathetically to
somebody else.   E ☐

Now tick the statement that comes closest to what you would have
said.

Now add anything else you would want to say about a 'good person'.

5   THE INFLUENCE OF SCHOOL

Some boys and girls of fifteen were asked if they thought they were
better now than when they came to their secondary school at eleven.

They all thought they were. So then they were asked if this improvement was due to the influence of school.

> I don't think the school makes you a better man: it just stops you going downwards.   A ☐

> I think the best thing about school socially is it helps you to mix with everybody.   B ☐

> We know a lot more than we did when we were eleven, and we've got our view-points on most things. When we were eleven we just took what teacher said for granted, now we argue it.   C ☐

Tick the statement you prefer.

Do you think your school has helped you to be a better person than you were four years ago?

How?

6   HOME AND SCHOOL

Do you find that the school and your parents often differ about what is right and wrong?

> No, they both don't want you to do what you want to.   A ☐

> They're trying to do what they think's best, but they don't give people a chance to say what's best.   B ☐

> Sometimes. If parents have got O levels and A levels they agree more than those that haven't.   C ☐

> It depends on the family, doesn't it? If you've got a family where there's bad manners and no respect, then the school's going to teach them differently.   D ☐

Tick the statement you prefer.

Do you feel that your home and your school really differ about the kind of person they want you to become?

7   PUNISHMENT

Do you think punishments have any effect on people?

> Yes, they make you *worse*. If the teacher shows

you up before the whole class you think, Oh blow 'er, I shall keep on talking. If she asks you nicely after the lesson to be a bit more quiet, you might.

A ☐

Do you think punishments are useful?

Yes, I think you've got to have them. If you had no punishments at all then school would be just a wild madhouse.

B ☐

Well, if you get punished I think it makes you more reluctant to work. But if you realize, your own self, in your own mind, that you must work, to get a good job, and everything, for your parents' sake, you do work. Better than being punished.

C ☐

Tick the statement you prefer.

Have *you* learnt anything because of being punished for a mistake?

Do you think some children *need* punishment?

8 RELIGIOUS EDUCATION

(*a*) What about RE, then? Has that had any influence on you?

No. I'm so bored I don't listen half the time.

A ☐

Loving thy neighbour, it's lovely that you should strive for it, but it's very difficult. It makes it easy to get so discouraged.

B ☐

A lot of people wouldn't get RE at home, so the school would be the place to learn it.

C ☐

I don't think you should have RE. I'm just wanting to learn maths and English and all that to help me in my future.

D ☐

Tick the statement you prefer.

Do you yourself get any ideas about moral goodness from RE?

(*b*) Is a good Christian different from just a good man who isn't a Christian?

I think a good person who isn't a Christian is a better person.

A ☐

A good Christian follows the Ten Commandments and then looks down on anybody else,
looks down their noses at them.   **B** ☐

To live happily and get on with people you must
behave in a Christian way.   **C** ☐

Tick the statement you prefer.

What do *you* think about the behaviour of Christians?

Note on the use of the questionnaire in schools

The main thesis of the book has been that the way boys and girls are
treated is of more importance in moral education than the way they
are talked to, or, worse, talked *at*. But a minor thesis has been advanced
that it *does* matter how they are listened to, and talked *with*. This
questionnaire could make the basis of a term's discussion, listening to
and talking with. A simple line of progress would be as follows:

1. Set the questionnaire. Read over the instructions, and renew the
   pledge to anonymity. They know that we can recognize hand-
   writing, but the pledge works like a mask at a *bal masqué*, and
   they will say their piece. Allow about forty minutes.

2. Present a list of 'wrong' activities they have suggested in 1a.
   Attempt some sort of categories (violence, crimes against property,
   sexual offences, and so on). Get the class to scale them, bad, worse,
   worst. Why? And are they *always* wrong?

3. Present the findings (i) from their papers (ii) from this book on
   question 1b. Thrash out the problem of lying in the light of the
   discussion on pp. 9-15. Try to form a general rule about lying.

4. Present the findings on shoplifting (1c), and raise the problems in
   the area of the so-called sanctity of private property: 'perks' in
   industry, requisitioning, fruit gardens, free rides on public trans-
   port, personal possessions in the family. Push the argument to the
   notion of personal value, and the tension between 'Persons matter
   more than possessions' and 'Possessions are an aspect of
   personality'.

5. Mercy-killing (2). Present the findings, having grouped the areas
   of response. Explore the situation in compassion for the victim
   and those who have to make the choice – there are occasionally
   mercy-killing trials in court. If the children get near to the heart
   of the matter, they might write a letter from a handicapped fifteen-
   year-old to the doctor who chose to let him live.

6. Drugs (3). There are two different sorts of issue here, one factual

and one moral. (i) What are the consequences of: tobacco, alcohol, cannabis, heroin? (ii) Has anyone the right to harm (*a*) other people (*b*) himself? The further question, Has the state (the school) the right to interfere (i) where there is argument about the degree of harmfulness and (ii) where the individual suffers alone? The first could lead to a discovery-project of fact-finding, with assistance from an expert (a doctor might be persuaded to come to the school), followed by an exhibition open to the school. The second could lead to an indeterminate argument, but in the course of it somebody will see that nobody really *lives* alone: No man is an island.

7. A good person (4). Again present the findings. Get the class to talk about people they have known, and thought of as good. Can they *generalize* about the goodness of people? What characters in the literature they have read were *really* good? In history? Can they guess at their secret?

8. The influence of school (5). Getting children to discuss their own education in the presence of one of their educators is a dangerous business. It may be handled with a certain detachment if the findings from this book (p. 54) are contrasted with their own, together with points made in the responses. The discussion can start from a confession that we all agree that schools are not yet perfect; so if *they* were planning a school (Utopia Comprehensive), what would they do, answering such questions as 'Should the school try to do more than "stop you going downwards"? If so, what? How?'

9. Home and school (6). Present the findings, and after discussing them, plan a meeting of a Parent-Teacher Association at Utopia Comprehensive, to be addressed by one, two, or three representatives of this form. What would they want to say in answer to 'They mean well, but ...' on p. 57?

10. Punishment (7). Discuss the findings. What punishment policy would you like to see in Utopia Comprehensive?

11. Religious education (8a). Present the findings. The traditional case has been that RE *does* promote a vision of goodness. Does this case hold? If not, where in the school do we learn what 'goodness' might mean?

12. Religious education (8b). Clear up just what a Christian *would* say about 'goodness'. *Is* there any difference from what anyone else would say?

Notes

1. James Hemming, *Problems of Adolescent Girls*, Heinemann 1960, pp. 88ff.

2. C. H. & W. M. Whitely, *The Permissive Society*, Methuen 1964, p. 18.

3. Ibid, p. 21.

4. Harold Loukes, *New Ground in Christian Education*, SCM Press 1965, pp. 86-7.

5. *Report of the Committee on Relations with Junior Members*, OUP 1969, p. 26.

6. J. P. White in *The Concept of Education*, ed. R. S. Peters, Routledge & Kegan Paul 1967, pp. 177ff.

7. Richard Hoggart, *The Uses of Literacy*, Chatto & Windus 1957, p. 98.

8. John A. T. Robinson, *Honest to God*, SCM Press 1963.

9. *Encounter*, September 1963.

10. David H. Hargreaves, *Interpersonal Relations and Education*, Routledge & Kegan Paul 1972, p. 331.

Index